If Only You Knew

You

Knew

JOHANNA THEA

ISBN 9781097290659

Cover photograph by CS Schalbroeck
www.krollekopproduction.com/

Typeset in London by Jeffrey Louis Salkilld

Printed in Great Britain by Amazon

Johanna Thea IMDB
https://www.imdb.com/name/nm4811231/

DEDICATION

To my grandmother Anna, friend and mentor. Who gifts
me her authentic self. Thus enabling me to be.

ACKNOWLEDGMENTS

Everything I do, would be impossible or at the least incredibly difficult without you all.

Andrea Kennedy
Anna Turakhia
Caitríona ní Catháin
Dani Schmidt
Gillian Boland
Greg Fitzgerald
Kathleen Fitzgerald
Ieva Junkure
Mairtín O'Catháin
Mary Wall
Meghan Treacy
Oisín Turakhia
Pesh Turakhia
Tiger Rudge

Special thanks to my editor Jeffrey Louis Salkilld without whom this edition would've remained an idea among a plethora. Your dedication, honesty and acumen in asserting your opinion with sensitivity to the subject matter and authors integrity, has set the bar so high I almost don't want to work with anyone else in this capacity.
One cannot express how beautiful it feels to be understood and have such great company to co-create with. May your talent bring you and others with whom you share endless joy and success! Also to all the amazing photographers whose work has made this a visual feast. Lastly, for those I haven't mentioned, you know how loved you are, it's just that your light seasoned my poetry and second book more perhaps, so it seemed strange writing your name here.

CONTENTS

INTRODUCTION

My fondest memories as a girl often involve books, watching films from Hollywood's golden era, being in nature and food (Mam is a wonderful cook!).

I read and wrote from around 3 years of age so while other children were learning to write, I was eagerly reading just for fun and libraries were my favourite spaces... often I'd want to take home too many books and it made me sad leaving some behind!

So I began writing long before I had reasons to, it is perhaps my first artistic experience of love. Yes, for what drove me to write wasn't the need to heal from trauma but my love for writing. The trauma was just the material from which the web was spun into beautiful patterns. Yet all was inspired through love.

My intention when writing this book was twofold; healing myself and helping others. I wanted to create something beautiful to share with the world out of all the trauma so I could let it go. Holding on to it all no longer served me.

I always look to Viktor E Frankl and other souls who came through horrific darkness, showing how we can all choose to shine.

Sometimes I chose to keep living because of others. Inside of me was either full of hurt or too confusing and had I been left alone it would've been too hard.

This book is a testament to how important others have been for my growth; from survival to thriving.

I hope once you learn my stories and see my wounds you'll grow too. There is always hope and no matter where we're at in life, love is always waiting for us.

Every single day I wake up knowing this truth and wanting to share it. Which is why this is the first book of many.

Enjoy! May 2nd 2019

1 IN THE ABSENCE OF TRAUMA

Too full of words to hear silence
and so we miss each other
Over and Over. Again.

Trauma can do strange things to a person. It can make you numb yet raw. Standing there so overwhelmed by the feeling of your innards having been kicked in, that you can hardly breathe. You are so stressed that knots have formed in your back and your shoulders are always tensed and held high.

This is so even when you get wasted, which is often enough to draw much attention to yourself. Trauma can do a great many things to a person. It can take away your sense of self. You can forget how to structure answers to any questions given to you by those who seek to understand your nature.

The problem with trauma is not only does it destroy the pleasure of sharing your journey, it makes you doubt parts of it were real, it makes you insecure in how much was caused by your involvement in that incident, in that happening. This tears at you, day in and day out.

You may choose your ways of answering questions when they reoccur frequently enough for you to be ready. It could be that you have learned how not to answer, deflecting, absorbing, using rhetorical answers, metaphors and questions which divert their attention as far away from you as possible.

For when you have no control over it, attention is like an oil torch flaming fire, the heat of which melts your skin, making it taut, so that it creases and folds still further and further inwardly. In the beginning you may well have screamed, but the effect of years of torture, or many torturous occurrences, reduces your reactions, so that now there are only two eyes which are glazed over.

You are not scared anymore or hoping any longer either. You know what is coming for this is the only absolute certainty in your life. You are sure that only more and more pain and suffering are inevitable. You know that you will hurt more and more and more. That it will never end. That you must try to end it. You must. You really must.

These are the thoughts which become the most pervasive in the end. Starving yourself is one way to help to numb all these feelings. Choice has such an element of adventure, of life and expectancy about it. It is a gift for those who gander gaily about their living, enjoying challenges and rising to meet them, head on.

Decision-making has elements of freedom to it, which are strong enough and carries just the right amount of force to diminish anyone who is uncertain already, to absolute confusion. It crushes anyone who is not themselves with the force of its weight, causing them to look around for other people's encouragement, support and help.

Feeling weak and uncertain they grow to ask those around them, is this the right decision? Should I do this? Such behaviours result in us losing our path and reclining deeply inside of ourselves, as we try, again and again, to engage in some sort of positive action.

The issue with this is, of course, that in order to

act, one has to know what one wants to do. Sometimes, when there are so many choices and we are given to believe that each and every single one has weight and matters a great deal, the hardest thing to do to make one. For we feel certain that once we do, should it be wrong, all is lost.

I understand this because I have been there and one of the things I did when I was there was to get high. High on alcohol, high on ecstasy, high on cocaine, high on whatever would make me higher.

While I was high, when I wasn't hugging, fucking or dancing, I was sharing my deepest darkest secrets. I was asking others questions about theirs. I felt myself trying, desperately, to find out where, why and how it had all happened and has it happened to you also? I found out it had and I found that you were also always seeking just like me.

I found so many truths, so much light. Yet still, that trauma etched itself into my skin, my behaviours and attitude. How I filtered the world and how I couldn't see, were all products of it. Yet there is more, yes, there is still so much more to tell you.

It was trauma that made me spend hours and hours and hours, staring out of my window at the road below. Recollecting the stories which I had heard about all of those people in this city who had been raped. There was one famed tale of a woman who was walking home and she gets attacked by this man.

He grabs her and shoves her to the ground. His hand is over her mouth and he is far stronger than she is. She squeals and tries to break free, but she's so much weaker than he. More so now that the fright has gotten hold of her and made her desperate, so her flailing arms don't carry much power, nor her movements much precision.

Yet, just in the nick of time a passer-by saves her. He is a young lovely man and he walks her home.

Unfortunately, when she gets to the door to take out her keys, the other man reappears and together they rape her and leave her there.

This is the story that I was told before leaving my city to move to this one. This is what haunted my mind as I looked out my window, being ever so careful to place the net back when anyone intimated that they might look up at me. It was fear, blind, stupid, all encompassing, terrible, terrifying, terrorising fear. It became me.

I was it, for I was nothing if not afraid. Trauma gifts you that. The terror lasts beyond all else. It enters into your psyche, punctuates all of your movements and traps you between them all. You are lost, always and forever, in amongst all the most decrepit and lonely views of yourself and the most hateful feelings about everything you could ever imagine. All is dark, darkened by that eternal burden of pain.

Trauma does other things too. It makes you feel like you must always be prepared to be hurt. This in turn leads you to thinking about disasters quite often. You think about them, then you replay them in your mind and gradually you grow used to the feeling that whenever something bad does happen, you can cope with it.

The thing is though, that in that time which you spend, running and rerunning ugly scenarios through your mind, you could already have made tea, hung out your washing and planned your week! You could have started writing that letter, found that person and had such splendid fun with them. You could have been partaking in so many activities. All now lost and buried beneath layers of ineptitude, fear, dread and shame. You are not enough. You are not.

The problem is though, that often these thoughts aren't quite conscious. You just slide into them, so to speak and when you do, you just let go of reality. They might be likened to your default thoughts. They run round and round your mind, always looking for your attention.

They are, after all, only neural pathways which you activated once in that specific way, which led to their announcing themselves in the form of a sentence. The automatic default streams of thoughts might sound something like;

"The train station will have shut their ticket offices by the time you get there. As a result you will have to talk your way out of a fine with the ticket inspectors."

The stream of thoughts comes with feelings of having done something terribly wrong. You feel guilty and small and ashamed of yourself. Your throat tightens and you may be unable to swallow. Your forehead creases, your hands clench into fists and your shoulders become rigid, fixed and taut.

Now, this is an actual scenario which you have to play out in your head. It is something which you choose to do, in order to prepare yourself for the worst. At least for me, this is what occurred. Over and over again these scenarios. What to do in the worst case scenario.

It is an endless stream of instances, your shoulders tightening each time they replay and your eyes gaze glazing over. It is a machine gun firing with thoughts of disaster, which means that it is the sound of the ocean, of laughter and of life happening around you, all disappears. All you can hear and all you can feel are those bullets as they pierce the air of your world, killing beauty and shattering life. Until it all just becomes a pile of meaningless dust on the floor beneath your feet.

Since ashtanga yoga I have noticed one considerable difference in this thread. That is that although it occurs at times, I am becoming far more cognizant of it. I do not completely enter into its stream.

Much in the same way as bulimia has left me, in the sense that there's no longer a battle over what to eat and when, nor how much because my body tells me all that, with trauma, there has recently been a flush of awareness.

So now, I actually get given the choice of whether or not to interact with these thoughts, with their incessant firing. I get to observe them as they rise from deep within me. I see their shape. I hold them above my head, rattle them a little, discover which noises they make, so that afterwards it is only my understanding of them which concerns me. I lose myself completely in discovering what they are made of, where they came from and why they are here.

It seems that, I may actually have made them myself at one time. That because I did not choose to actively get rid of them, somehow, they have always remained with me, like a stray animal following you home. So too, in the process of clearing one's mind, there is oh so much garbage to be found which has been picked up along the way.

Garbage which trauma consolidates and refuses to let you see. Garbage which looks just like the names and faces of all of those people you see so often. The ones who hate and despise you, or worse, those who accept and love you even though you're so stupid and dumb.

It is trauma which paints these people thus and it also that which makes you so damn certain of who you are to them, because you can be no other way. That is it for now. You are that. Although there may well have been a time when you were otherwise, it is so hard to discern now, that you may as well accept what has come to be accepted as true of late.

This is that you are exactly as you feel and know and understand yourself to be. It means that if others don't get that, if they do not understand the ways in which you are, it is not a challenge to how you know yourself to be at all. Rather, it is part of their misunderstanding of you.

Somehow they have come to understand and know you differently to how you actually are. This is why regardless of how often you might be challenged by a view which does not assimilate quite so easily into your own view of yourself, it does not matter. All views are disregarded; especially those which are positive and good, for only you can truly know yourself, surely?

Only you understand the depths from which your own dawning perception of yourself may arise. It is a well founded vision, borne of scars and pain which you must have needed. Filled with others treatment of you, which you must have drawn through who you actually are. It makes sense like this, logically, otherwise why did it all happen?

The truth is that, if you question this reasoning, you may have to actually start listening to something other than the pains which they have caused. You may have to start again and with starting again, comes that fear that you may get hurt more than ever before and proven right anyway.

So you see how it is! What is the point? You have exhausted yourself once more, without ever actually having to do anything at all. So that you sink back down into the depths of yourself and your very own perceptions.

It is in this way that traumas' ripples are felt. Like slices of consciousness, which are at once masked by the imposition of the unreality of their very selves. So you too are masked. So too are you smothered in tape of your own untoward suppositions concerning yourself. So too then, are you given to unfeeling and made to escape from the reality of your being.

Perhaps even those aspects of you which are true and real and good? Well, who knows about the latter, but at least that part of yourself which you know to be yourself, is left behind, smothered from within and smouldering gently in itself. Trauma has forgiven it the burden of the expression of its existence and with that, so too forgiven you so much of your own life. Trauma has whipped you until you bled and forgotten that very thing which has caused you so much pain.

Trauma has your eyes wide open and gaping at the

world. It means that even at the slightest sound, they may widen suddenly, with your soul peering out while trying not to move. Trauma makes you hold your breath in.

When somebody has difficulty in breathing you know it can be because of something external. Something scary which has marked and scarred them so deeply, that now they cannot move without it. It carries itself with them, perching just in front of their lips, ready to leap within at the slightest opportunity. On such occasions it is best not to move too much, not to make anyone too aware of their being any life within. It is better that way and it is much, much safer also.

Something happened to me which disrupted my breathing too. Something so harsh that it completely melted my exterior. I wonder still if that wasn't a blessing in so many ways. I wonder if those people who caused me so much harm, myself included, weren't just participating in some obtuse way of carving out the centre of my being, so that it would become illuminated through the clarity that lay between it and all others.

I wonder that before I arrived here, at this space and time, I didn't already know how hard it would be, not the actual experiences, but to come back from them. Darkness speaks a language which also introduces the soul to itself. It is not that darkness and light are opposites, they are the exact same material from different perspectives and it is the emotion through which one sees which introduces the change.

The fact that I am thinking of you now, makes me not really want to go into this feeling associated with trauma. Something else is happening instead and it is as if I am looking at it, yet it is not really affecting me. I have somehow found a space called love at last; a place where there is absolute trust and here, I can allow myself to look and see quite clearly, whatever is in front of me.

Not only that, but I am also absolutely free to let it go. To let all of my fears, anxieties, troubles, anticipations and all that stuff, go. I am here, living wild and free in this moment and it is pure and right and true. It is so very beautiful; really, I cannot even tell you how good this feels. Suddenly this returning to trauma is a cathartic event, an act of purification and yes, somehow it all becomes such an absolute blessing.

So you see how it is? Now I am ready to be an actress, so that now I am indeed just that. Truly, before, it was somehow hard to engage with all those feelings, they weren't yet within my power and I had no control over them either. Yet now that I have arrived and become how I am feeling, this feels truly great.

It is like that moment when peace descends as you are looking out over the ocean, because while you know that eventually you may die in its arms, as you are going to die anyway, it does not matter who takes you any longer. At that thought, you are smiling and it becomes an especially powerful thing.

It is liberating, not knowing exactly what this beautiful force is to become to you. I am wondering that love isn't like this, that you don't eventually give yourself over entirely to so many things when you are able to understand, that the only way of losing anything, is in not doing exactly that.

Trauma has taught me many things too, like how to let go of stuff and also how to see. It gave me the freedom and insight to not have to know why, but to trust that very delicate spark which flutters in your stomach from time to time.

It was so extreme in fact, that although I am still as sensitive as I was then, I can somehow remove myself from the painful aspects of its awareness. It helped me to understand my strength and know that I can survive and endure many, many things, but that I do not want to. It also gifted me the understanding that not only do I not want to; I do not want others to suffer.

Trauma taught me all of that, but it took around

ten years before I could see beyond the pain. Ten years of intermittently being traumatised by myself or others, ten years trying to get out, a couple of years of quick progression and now, finally, we are here.

My life experiences stretch in so many different directions and they feel in many ways unreal. I have the greatest insights imaginable because of these experiences. I have insights because of past pains caused, because of being made to feel things that many people do not.

For example, ten years ago I was made to sleep in the garage by my alcoholic mother. She would fly into rages with me, which I did little to stop. We would argue, my words came from both fear and anguish, for anger feeds well on those ingredients. She, being smaller and older and drunk, would come towards me, dragging me by my clothes, hair, or the flesh of my arms and eventually manage to push and shove me outside.

I suppose now that I was a nonconformist. The truth is, that I have only just realised that now. At the time I was angry and I would march away when she wouldn't answer my knocks. At some times, I wouldn't even knock, that's how stubborn I was! I would instead march off down into our garage. Lifting the door, shuddering in the cold night air, I would clamber into a chair. I would place some cardboard boxes on top of it, trying to shield the wind; I think that there were some cushions there too.

The thing is that I would become so, so emotional. The tears would fall hard and fast and I grew to hate each one as they attracted the cold to my skin. I remember also hating the need to pee and willing it to disappear because I really didn't want to uncurl myself.

I hated myself, for being born and I hated my body for living on in spite of the pain and discomfort. I think it was Kahlil Gibran who said that you will find the same things you once wept for, are the same things you now rejoice at. This is my truth and journey. It was a horrendous period of my life. I was battling on every front and became exhausted and nothing mattered.

In the end I was a liar, but you see, what are lies to someone who hasn't got anything to live for? I lied for attention which my desperate soul thought was love. I lied because I wanted another mother to love me, never realising that my own did, it was just that she was sick.

I was sick too then. I was lost and sick, cold, alone and shivering in the garage of my own personal hell. I carried hell within me for many years in the expectation of it being pervasive. I would like to apologise to anyone I burnt with my internal fire raging. I didn't mean you any harm; I just didn't care enough about anyone or anything to prevent it. I do now though.

So there I am in the garage, crying and shivering and hoping our cats had found warmer places to sleep. I was trying to sleep to forget about the cold and I also wanted to forget about everything that had happened. My brain burned with the painful sting of rejection and I knew I was worthless.

I remember with great clarity the urgency with which I wanted so badly to forget. This I do recall. The cold chilled me to the bone and I woke often throughout the night, shivering and numb. My anger, pain and sense of disdain and disgust were immense. I carried those around with me until I was able and ready to face them and let them go.

Now they are gone, for I can walk away from both people and feelings of guilt, shame and fear quite easily. Until it was okay though, I clung to them, so used was I to how they had made me feel it felt comfortable to be with them. They housed me and I felt so weak and alone that these were all I had to cling to. I felt so alone and lost; that all these dark feelings were all I had left to cushion me.

My habitat was a sad, cold, lonely, horrible, dark world, filled with so many obstacles. Getting out of bed every single day was such a struggle because I couldn't see or feel and didn't want to either. I was a prisoner of darkness and a slave to both my fears and all that hurt me.

What I have realised now, is that my mother was sharing her world with me. It was not then, nor ever shall be, my world. I am not sure what has made her so very scared and angry. I don't know why she had no self control, or even acceptance. I may never know, or I may come to realise over time.

What little I have come to understand of my mother, has enabled me to release myself from the prison of misunderstanding. I am finally free from all impositions. I stand alone and that is usually okay. The sound of the wind rustling through the leaves soothes my soul and appeases whatever kind of anguish comes along. For I know that we are all here together in this life.

Trauma has vanished and left me with life. I hold her hand, embrace her body, dip my fingers deep inside of her warmth and enjoy sharing the pleasure and joy of that exchange, wherein she both recognises the life in me and I also accept the 'me' in life. I am alive and I am not afraid to explore. This is what happens when there is the space for intimacy. It has indeed already happened and it is such a joy!

Trauma can be a good thing, she says to me as we are seated across from each other in the bar. Her deep chocolate brown eyes are beautiful whirling pools, within which I somehow find peace, joy and renewal. I have just explained to her that I was writing about trauma when she texts me and thereafter it became about understanding the benefits of trauma.

In truth, absolutely everything is beneficial and there is nothing in life which we cannot use to our advantage. There is nothing that cannot gift us deeper understanding, insight, or some purer element of truthfulness. The other thing which is remarkable about trauma is how it tears you away from life. It actually gifts you a perspective which is forever far removed from the common limited and more narrow one and enables you to see things which before, you couldn't.

It also blinds you to certain things which are apparent to those not affected by trauma. There are certain obvious truths which have to be spelled out to you for you to see them. I think they call this common-sense; I was too blinded emotionally to understand much of it, even having been told on countless occasions.

People have mocked me for this my whole life, some in jest and others not. Sometimes part of the common-sense I lack is to know that others tease you to play with you, because they like you. It was a tool my mother used to poke me and whip me mentally with. I know that when it stops hurting entirely I am healed, like when I stopped flinching when people moved suddenly, I had healed from the fear of physical violence, something which brought a great sense of shame.

Trauma single-handedly takes away your ability to rely on yourself. You can no longer ascertain easily what it is that you are feeling exactly and why. You become hyper vigilant and overly sensitised. The effects of trauma are such that both your actions and reactions become totally illogical and emotionally based.

It is the thing which makes everything ambiguous feel bad and makes waiting feel like you are being drawn out until something bad happens. Perhaps something worse than before, or worse than imagined. It is that thing which keeps you stone still and stagnant, when you should be moving and forces you to keep going even when you are far beyond being exhausted. It is among the most difficult cages to escape from.

It ruins your perception of time, which only results in true freedom when you are conscious enough to realise that you still need some rest. However, what you shall find eventually is that once you look into your own trauma and choose to see what it means exactly and how that meaning has come about, you have an unspoken treasure.

You have the gift of insight into people's pain and the realisation of it as totally separate from your own. This in turn, gifts you the freedom to walk away, to say no and to remove yourself from certain circumstances which are not fulfilling your needs.

Additionally, you can learn more subtle forms of communication, which are entirely inaccessible to a world of other people. It is also now within you to remain patient in the face of unbearable inconsistencies in your life and equally, adjust to ways of being imposed on you by external factors and circumstances.

Also, because you have had to endure the burden and intense fires of pain before, you will now be able to endure far more. The only pitfall here of course, is enduring certain annoyances and unpleasant feelings and ways of being for longer than is necessary.

Just remember, that everything which you have experienced and shall ever experience has its' place and space. Life is a broad spectrum of these experiences, within which you are seated in the centre. Losing linear time and ingrained and conditioned perspectives due to traumas impositions are all gifts for you to cultivate.

Do so and your perennial garden shall blossom and bloom, along with all the love and joy which you have inside. Not just as a survivor, but as somebody who had chosen to thrive, against all odds and regardless of your prior circumstances and ways of being.

At the end of the day, the only thing we really have to get over, is our selves. Once we see this, the most remarkable things are capable of happening, as a result of and yet also, In the Absence of Trauma.

2 THE BITCH

The drunken love of time
moves me
and I am
Beaten. Apart. By your love.

She came to us in a time before money. It was a time of absolute innocence, when the price of things didn't matter to us quite as much as the understanding that everyone had exactly what they needed.

It was just this which took us into her arms. Into the arms of a killer of innocence. She took us and placing her arms around us all together, gathered us so closely. She was all we could see and all we understood that we were feeling and soon we forgot about all that time without her there.

She gathered us up together, just like that and kept squeezing us, until we could hardly breathe. Right then when we thought we would pass out from the lack of oxygen, she let us go. Brushing her hand delicately along our faces and grinning gently, she told us that we were indeed the bravest people whom she had ever known.

Her grin broke into a laugh, as she threw her head

backwards and allowed all of the air which she alone had stolen from inside of our lungs and hearts and souls, to cascade through her and it made the most awful sound.

It was not the sound of awakening, but the sounds of darkness, not just one, but many crushed together and mixed in with all kinds of sin and mischief. Afterwards, she slapped one of us playfully a little too hard and when we yelped, it was apparent she was salivating from the look in her eyes. Some people feast on pain.

We began to forget about her every time she would leave. But invariably she would always come back. She would always return with stressed out, knotted and hunched over shoulders and her eyes gleaming.

She would walk towards us making the peace sign with her fingers and while the others hardly noticed, it was this which eventually made me relax into her trap. She had many ways of trapping us too. She simply loved to play. It was not at all a good thing to be speaking with her and there was no single part of her which wasn't looking for a way to twist things. She enjoyed twisting your words as much as your perception and she was equally as good at both.

It was when she moved in that things started to lose the charm inherent in them. The wood which once seemed to have aged and retained its character, suddenly held the appearance of something which had at once been too well used and too little tended to. The cracks which once gave it a sense of history, just made it look old and the whole room where she stayed took on the form of something which was dilapidated.

She broke the peace with her broken heart and the generous hearts of the many gave her exactly what she wanted and yet so very little of anything which she may ever need. It was an exchange which was purposeful and apparently lucrative, but she still foraged for the cheapest pizzas and drank cheap beers in bars with people whom she did not know and never could.

She still slept with many, she still wanted to be fucked harder and harder and perhaps she always would. It was a condition of the depravity of her soul, the ways in which she could find to express her needs. The ways in which she could never ever stop trying to do just that.

She would destroy anybody and anything which tried to get in her way, because there was nothing which she could not have, except the one thing which she really wanted. She came as every single wanderer comes, from a time and place which remain unspoken and unspeakable.

When she did speak it was never to give you anything, except exactly how she was feeling at that exact moment of time. It was not to share in her experiences, all of her emotions remained trapped. All of her truths about who she loved and how deeply. All of the sounds which wandered past her wandering soul. All of the tastes which she felt to have more or less of.

Indeed, all that makes up a character evaded the spaces which she shared with others and instead she made it her business to extract what was theirs from them. She would wind them up, spit them out, play with them, love them, hate them or do whatever it was that she felt was necessary in order to get them to do whatever she pleased.

It was this that she enjoyed. It was only this that she hungered after, it was this which made her whine and cry, demand and react, it was only ever this. It was that she was a princess who would continue stamping her feet until all and sundry obeyed her command.

If they did not acquiesce easily and with grace, she would demand of them more than they could ever give and when they collapsed exhausted and broken to the ground, then she would grin and do her dance.

She liked to dance. She liked to dance and sing and to pretend that she was totally in charge of all the sounds she made and that it was she who commanded them through her, from wherever they came initially.

When she was singing and dancing, she was also

always thinking of this and a dimple would appear. Firm and solid in her right cheek. The trouble was of course, that nobody stays dancing forever, there are times when one grows weary and the words get lost. Then the real self comes out, the real person and all their goodness, or otherwise. This is the worst case scenario really, for who can vilify and fight against somebody who is as human as oneself? How does one truly know the extent of their deviancy and horrid intent? Except through some mad and blinding intuition of just that?

It is not that she is evil you see, it is only that her will has nothing to soften it. No love, no intimacy and nobody there beside her to gently hold her hand, who she is not already using. She is alone. Absolutely alone. Alone.

She is tired, but you will not see her fall. It would not matter even if her body in its exhaustion failed to operate properly, because her will would still drive her forwards. She can not stop. There is no force known to man which can make her stop. There is no one who loves her enough to try. So you see the tragedy in it also?

When she comes, she sucks the purity and innocence from the place, until nothing is left but darkness. The inner darkness she feels is then matched by the home she's made into a house filled with rooms, devoid of laughter and light, though there may be sunshine outside.

She turns girls into women and what was free into something which can be profited from. She comes and takes it all and makes it her own somehow, yet she has absolutely nothing. Nor can she have, until she lets every single thing that she has ever worked so hard, at destroying herself for, gone.

Until then she shall always be self destructing and she will always be driven. Until loves hand comes and takes hers, she will always be alone. Until she is able and ready and willing to hold loves hand back, all is lost. She cannot ever move from the cycles inherent in the movement of her own will. Within her movements, she has stagnated and now there is nowhere left for her to go and she is hungry.

She is hungering for all the things she can see around her, which she cannot touch or feel. She is hungry for love, for its depth and texture. For how it brings meaning into every single day and the ways in which it caresses you while sleeping. She's hungry for the way the light from the others gaze penetrates her own. For how their look and them looking makes her feel. She is hungry and surrounded by food which she cannot eat and even when she tries her hardest, which she cannot get nourishment from.

So this is the situation as it stands. The bitch has emerged from deep within herself and chosen to show different aspects of that same self to different people at different times. She has judged and guided their reactions well enough to be able to impose her will upon them, yet she has not yet won.

The truth is that all that she does is solely in order that each and every individual within that house may choose to expose themselves to her, of their own free will. So she finds a weak spot in each and she plays with it.

Gently at first and then gradually with a perseverance and insistence with which to aid distracting herself from her hunger. It is this hunger which gets channelled into these other activities and it is in this way that she finds her pleasure.

She eats people's energy and attention and uses whatever they give her to create a soft and gentle noose around their neck. She takes people who like to be enslaved and makes pets of them. She has all sorts of creatures under her control and when she manages to get them to enjoy her taste she allows it to linger before moving in such a way as to drag them along behind her.

She creates fantastic pictures and images in the minds of others. She sows seeds and tends to them, feeding and watering them as often and as well as is possible. Having planted seeds and imposed her perspective upon their keepers, without their direct knowledge or control, but with gradual gradients of consent, she uses this to its' fullest advantage.

The only problem with her method of course, is that it is tiring, for she has absolutely no energy of her own. So she is entirely reliant on the energy and emotion of others to feed herself. This makes her absolutely powerful and beyond control or reproach in certain instances and completely surrounded by the absence of everything alive in others.

Her reliance spreads to encompass everything that is going on around her. If you are someone within her control, then you are trusted, for she can determine exactly what it is that you are doing and why. If however, you are one who lies outside of her domain, she treats you with absolute disdain.

She enjoys whipping you with her words and actions, enforced through the burning desire to have you under her control. Chastising you until you have cause to ask yourself why this woman is determining that so many aspects of what you are saying and doing are inferior to hers.

Until, one day, you find yourself wondering if she might be right after all and it is then that she has got you. In that instant, in that moment when you begin questioning and doubting yourself, she has got you in her grasp. You are hers for keeping then and there's nothing which you can do about it.

She has, through confusing and blinding you emotionally to all responses to which you are used, caused you to doubt your very own self. In that exact moment when you doubt yourself, you are lost and she is the light. For it is she that has cast you into the darkness and so only she too, who has that power to set you free.

Now, there are many, many ways through this

passage of time, reactions, play and battling, to be able to see beyond it all and into the eyes of the stranger who faces you. I can only describe my way to truth, without imposing that as the only way, but only in the bid to advocate the fact that you can indeed find your way to light alone. It is not easy, but it does not take very long. All that you have to remember is that it is not a fight; it is rather a process of letting go.

For you must let go of enough of yourself and of the weight which you are carrying in order to be able to fully see. This is that which is happening and is the only truth. The reality is that the only way forward is through you and that the only way through yourself is through letting go.

In tending to what you have kept, in looking at and appreciating it fully, in holding it delicately in your arms and kissing it on its' gorgeous forehead, before choosing consciously to just enable its' disappearance from your life. You are setting it free, much in the way we are continuously setting everyone around us free.

Yet still, even when we think that setting them free is within our control, all that we are actually doing is accepting them fully into love. This is that process of which I speak. This is the letting go; it is the way that we are given to love and to loving continuously until we are completely freed.

I guess the best thing about the bitch's arrival is that she has enabled us to see ourselves. She carries with her something of a torch. Somehow, through her shit stirring she makes all the bad shit come to the fore. We get to see the worst possible aspects of ourselves and then let these go. We get to be freed of all pretension, to forego our misunderstandings between, among and within ourselves and choose instead to observe, to actually observe ourselves as we truly are.

This is the truth. That every single person is given to us as somewhat of a gift and that that is why you are not only a bitch, you are our bitch. You belong to the universe as much as our angels and all that lies in between. Without you there is no movement forward and many things stagnate. When one lives with you for long enough, one understands the complexities of your behaviour and that part of what motivates you is what moves us all, desire. It is the fear factor in you which makes you darker than us. Not that all of us, just two.

The other is also moved by fear more than love, but that is a condition of her environment and those factors which are all beyond her control. For she cannot, in all honesty, but worry and be fearful. Her fearfulness comes from the knowledge that her father is about to die and the awareness of that, permeates through to every single aspect of her being. But I digress, for this is not her story.

The one of whom we speak is far from evil. It is just that she has such great determination, that it absolutely replaces all of her other faculties. It might be that she is indeed so dog headed that nothing but whatever she wants is good enough. It may also be that she is more aware of power and control at the expense of all else than anyone I have ever come across in my entire life. At the very least, that I am aware of.

Getting what you want at all expenses is usually some form of ignorance on the part of the seeker. I do not mean that one ought not have desire, or want with all of ones being to accomplish much and that this cannot drive and motivate us. It does, it has and it always will, even as regards parenthood and schooling there is a strong and powerful element of just this force at play.

Nay, I am not saying anything against this force as such; rather, what I am saying is that there are many other forces also. That the awareness of when one's own desires and needs may cause harm to another, either emotional, mental or any sort of pain, ought to encourage one to refrain from pushing too hard.

It is just that when one has awareness of all the creatures around oneself, when one loves with one's own heart and feels with it and is given to understanding that we all have the power within us to harm or to heal, such hard line decisions may be made, but not kept. That is the truth.

The bitch was in my dream last night again. I do not remember the dreams that came before, but I do know that they have existed. In this one we were in this great big white room, perhaps with those light brown wooden floor boards, I really am not certain, but it felt like one of those old activity buildings, in spite of it being bathed in luminous light.

She was sat on the floor and I was dreadfully drawn to her, yet somehow to communicate with her was so difficult. I felt strongly that I wanted to connect with her and to make her feel safe, but I could not move towards her. There was also someone else there beside her, who seemed like a woman but felt like a girl and she was standing next to her the whole entire time and I noticed, but hardly. Much as one might notice a speck of dirt in ones tea whilst speaking with a friend, or indeed the spinach between the teeth of one's friend also. It was indeed strange.

I don't think that anything could have protected me from the pain of what happened. It was not a heart pain, exactly, although it did come from there, it was the sudden, yet soft and gentle pain of realisation. That sensation when one is piecing all the parts of a certain occasion together and then at last comes across its' meaning in the process, but of course, one was almost totally unaware prior to this.

It was the sensation that led to my staring and not quite being able to let go with my eyes nor my awareness as I understood. It was the girl who would help her in the end. The tall girl with the short hair, who would walk with her through her life and into the seat of her Ph.D. It was simply this.

I had no occasion to frown, in truth one only wants for those one loves to be happy and well looked after and safe. None of these could not have been completed by this girl, but you see, it was still not me. For the first time in my life the understanding arises, that sometimes you are simply not the best person to walk beside another and if you truly love them then you do not feel bereft.

It is not my fault that I have found myself loving some of the most horrible people. It is only because I can see their hearts under the myriad ways in which they are stained and more than anything I wish them release from their pain. More than anything, I wish them freedom and love and happiness.

Yet I cannot help them at all it seems. Rather you simply are able to watch and see. You just allow it to flow past you, because to stop any kind of continuation of their growth would not only be selfish, but unloving and we are anything but that. It was a tender occasion indeed.

Perhaps the dreaming came as closure. For, as regards the events of the meeting that occurred in my room, it could not have ended in a more beautiful and peaceful way, however I did feel that it all lacked closure. I wanted badly for somebody to walk out of my room with her. To tell her that it is okay, that it's all going to be okay and that it just takes time. I wanted not to have to let her go, but I did. I had to.

It had to end like that in that moment, or else none of it would have made sense. It could not have been counteracted, counterbalanced or cushioned. It was of utmost importance that she was able to crash deeply inside of herself and so I did let her go. I had no choice because unfortunately, she had chosen me to fight against and it was I who came to represent all that she wanted and could not get in that house. In many ways it is only through that ability to let her go, that I have learned how to let all of the rest of them go also.

Everyone else has to be let go of now too. It is just like that in life. Once you get used to the benefits of not holding on, then that is exactly what occurs. You let it all slide, you release yourself into each and every situation and you enable each and every situation to release you.

I did not know how to let go before. It is something that wounded me in the past. I thought that in letting go you could be lost, I did not realise that only through actually letting go, do you fully accept somebody else into your being.

Essentially, you are saying, you are telling them, that you trust them. That you do not mind if they do not come back, for that is not even the point. Rather, that you can let them go and should they choose to come back, you shall always be there to welcome them with open arms. That is power and a love which is unconditional and true and that is what has happened to me in my life.

I am a wide open gaping chasm of love. When they say that love hurts it is absolutely true, but not in the basic sense of that word; hurt. It is not that you are arguing and fighting all of the time. It is not even that you are so jealous, or afraid of losing them, or tired of your journeying together that it causes you pain. It is none of these things.

It is only that you not only have no expectations, but that your door remains eternally open to and for them. This means that you never let go of their hand, or of loving them, or of accepting all that they are and have done and shall be. That you may have to keep on letting them go again and again and again, but that these things do not matter at all. It does not matter.

What hurts is keeping yourself so very open that you never ever close. It does not only hurt, for loving brings about the greatest element of peace and sanctity. It blesses you both. It is courage and fire, it is introversion and truth, it contains every possible element of yourself and of them also, yet it does not ever bind you or them. It is about their continual release, to remap the ether, to scope out what is happening, to connect at different levels, to expose oneself over and over again to varying degrees of vulnerability and to let all of these things flow. Love hurts because you love so much and so deeply and so entirely and all at once that it feels at times that there is nothing of you left but that love. It may indeed be so.

What that bitch taught me in her agony and pain, in her deciding to circumscribe and twist herself and all of us also, was ingenious. In her journeying towards dictatorial actions, in her deploying many forms of manipulation and devising means of destroying bonds and perceptions, she taught me that the highest truth is actually love. For love enables us to reveal all of ourselves and there is nowhere that is not safe when you are in love.

For being love is the highest form of communion and in this sense it is the highest form of power, in that it is recognised by all beings as simply that. The bitch taught me how to love and accept myself and others in a way that is unconditional, simply because I accepted her, in spite of her behaviours. In many ways, it was an acceptance like that of the darkness, because it is alien to yourself and unknown and somehow too, will never be known.

Yet, this experience is one that enabled me to lay bare in front of myself and others and simply say, this is I. It is not that the entire scenario was caused by me, or was for me, or that I feel that I am the centre of everyone else's universe. It is not that. However, I have accepted myself as that for me only. I am one who works from the inside out now.

The bitch was the last person in my external reality to whom I was drawn to making my ruler. To whom I wished to bestow all forms of glorification, power, and adoration. Indeed, to whom I really wanted to gift my trust, to lead me so that I maybe, would not have to lead myself. It was my childish foray into dependency and I am grateful it suffered death. She cut all of the strings of attachment with her words and crushed all of my expectations and desires underfoot, smilingly and in doing so, she has set me free.

I am so grateful for all the bitches in my life. You are the result of millions of years of evolution and are extraordinarily astute and fantastic in all that you do. I thoroughly enjoy your company and dare I say it, I always will enjoy it, most especially its' brevity. Equally shall I thoroughly enjoy that it will not be me who walks with you through your lives. I shall not be the one eagerly trying to communicate with you and connect.

Invariably also, it shall not be me who is dragged about by the hair behind your scurrying feet. Nor I, who gets damaged by your fantastically contrived and ever sharpening claws. You will not get to spit into my face, crush my hopes and dreams underfoot, nor bark at me for not obeying your orders. It is only for your bitches to do those things and I, my darling girl, am anything but your bitch.

3 CO-CREATORS OF OUR SILENCE

Take my addressing you
with a pinch of salt
Lest cunning sour
my mirth extends
your hearts rhythms

I want you to come here. I want you to come here now and cupping my face in the palm of your hand, kiss my wrinkled nose. I want you to touch me, deeply, not just that superficial kind of grasping that comes so easily to so many! No.

I would like for you to choose to reach deep inside of me and taking my hands in yours, ease me gently outwards. I want for you to be here with me, by my side when I am falling. I do not want for you to feel that you have to catch me, you do not. I do not want for you to feel obliged even to help me up, for I feel certain that your just being around, is sufficient for my getting back up again. It has always been thus and thus it shall always remain.

I want for you to sit down here beside me and share in this silence. I have willed some of it, you have willed some more, so together we get to share in its happening, as co-creators. I want that for us. For our love to be something of whatever we both endeavour to share. For our truth to be shared between us and within our shared spaces. I would like that very much.

I would also like to see into your eyes. I would like to sit right beside you and spend absolute hours just looking into your eyes. As if I were here to save you through looking and you were here to save me through looking too. That would be nice!

It is not that either of us needs to be saved exactly, only that we are choosing to believe that we can be. It is nice at times, to leave the thoughts of the world far behind us. It seems only fair to do just this.

I would like for us to be sat together, looking deeply into each other's eyes and simply feeling that moment with all of its power. It is a wonderful thing knowing exactly what you want and an even better thing getting it.

I think that the most important part though, is that you get here on time. I am not certain when that is, but it is totally down to you to organise yourself around that happening. I am somehow feeling that you do want me, that you have wanted me for quite some time. That you are hyper aware of all that you are doing. I have this inkling that you also know that timing is absolutely everything. Therefore, we both know the same things.

Of course, you have given me no foundation upon which to build this perspective. It is not actually a perspective as such; it is somewhat of an implicit understanding. You enter my dreams and psyche, just as you exit them, without the slightest warning, yet still it is all making absolute sense.

I wrote you quite some time ago when I was feeling like a loser because of my lack of cash. Of course now those feelings and thoughts would simply never even enter my mind. Yet they did then, I have not come across such extreme poverty in my own life, for such a very long time you see.

Also, I suppose, retrospectively, something deep inside of me was breaking. Somehow there was a distinct lack of trust. I am so glad that you were there to guide me through that. You didn't offer emotional support, but the mere fact that you remained around was quite cool. I am certain that you have not gone forever. You may even be thinking of me now, why wouldn't you be?

I hate to say this. It is beyond me how I can admit this even to myself, but my soul knows you and waits for you and sometimes it finds itself looking deeply into your eyes, even in your absence.

I want you to know that I support you doing whatever makes you happy and that right now, in spite of my romanticism, I must force myself to move on. I refuse to wait sat on the highway of life with a flat tyre, choosing never to learn how to fix it, in case you come along to help. Instead, let me say that my soul loves you and shall wait for you until it doesn't any longer.

Meanwhile, I am here learning how to fix my tyre and every now again, those passing stop and offer me assistance. Some bring laughter, joy and stories and others refreshments and encouragement, some cast aspersions in my direction and make me glad inwardly not to be like them.

All add to my life and as the hours are passing I am more and more grateful for the flat tyre and less and less concerned that it should ever bring you back. Rather now, I feel destined to happen upon my journey towards my destination, that the pause was so I could know how I felt and also, that feelings are not complete, nor stagnant, nor even indicative of any particular outcome.

I have left all my belongings behind me now and am adventuring along the highway of my life without a care in the world. I am surrounded by love of those old and new, challenges bring peace and joy and I wish all these blessings on you too, without the pain of our remembrance pickling it all, with its pangs.

Also, more than anything I am looking forward to our meeting a little further along the way, perhaps, both with room for chats and looking, listening and learning from one another. I do not know why I know you so well and trust our journey so much and feel that we ourselves as well as that which we do are so fully intertwined, but I do.

I cannot explain how I am feeling, except to say that I remain here where you left me, even as you found me, as you are, because, you see, we have found each other on that exact premise alone, as our very own true selves and this is what makes it all so fantastically exciting!

Knowing that you exist and feeling safe in that fact, brings such a smile to my face and heart and mind and soul, I cannot tell you. Perhaps one day though, I shall be able to show you, for you might just choose to see it for yourself and maybe we shall also find that together, we are co-creators of our silence.

4 WHAT IS GIVEN

I can't feel my heart
For beating
Between my eitherways

Life is too important for us not to be ourselves. I have realised at last what the trouble is. It is in being alone. It is not the workload for university exactly, although I do struggle and fight against that which I do not enjoy doing and most especially, that which I am made to do. I struggle like an animal caged, trapped in its own idea of itself as being bound. That is what I have just realised.

Freedom is not a concept; it exists, even as we do and such as we are, freely. I want to reach out to you to tell you that I understand, that I finally get it, what it means to be free, yet I can't. Now that my illusion is shattered and I can see that I was just another girl to you then, now that I understand that for you I was never really the one, I cannot offer you my hand for my heart is broken.

I am alone and sitting and writing and I know now that I shall forever be alone and it is this that enables me to truly and fully, be and feel this pain. It is not that dramatic kind of pain, it is a feeling borne only out of the heart. It is not rejection though, nor loss, nor any of the

32

billions of other things that you might suppose it to be. It is only understanding. It is the root of my understanding of my own aloneness and the pain is my tearing away at the idea of anything else.

Pain comes from the breaking apart of an illusion, I can see that now, I even feel it in my heart and its' agony. I shall reach out to you no more and we have left each other, bereft. I could speak of all of the thoughts which I have had, so many ideas and imaginings, I could and that would be okay, but there is no need for all of those things now. The time for our discussions has passed, I do not know why I thought we belong together, I believed in so many things.

Now I see inside my mind, at how the seeds you planted came and took nourishment from all those lies and how I had an entire forest in my brain when you left me. It is only recently that the fires left, which enabled all of them to burn down and for the ashes to return to the soil where I could nurture it to grow new things, new ideas and new love. It is only now.

I fell in love with the ideas you gave me and in the interim I lost so many people, because all the while my heart belonged to you and now I know why. It is a shame because you did not love me, but hey, that is not your fault. You were trying to set me up with your friend, when I thought you were actually sending in someone to spy on me for you.

I was far too busy over thinking things to be free just to see and maybe I needed you then. It may be that you entering into my life, as and when you did, was a requirement. Some sort of prerequisite for whatever is to come, with my imminent graduation from university and freedom.

Well, I now know that I am always free and have been so forever, yet still I cannot move away from my laptop, in my room, with my things and I have not written such an amazing essay as I would have liked. It does not matter though. I will write it. I will stay up for days and days and make it as magical and clever and informative and refreshing as I can, for my professor and I will be happy.

My heart hurts. When you are growing into who you are, no one ever tells you that it will hurt from time to time and that that pain is good. It is because you have learned something essential to your being. It is because you are about to heal. It is good. I must remember to tell my children that part, I think that they shall remember it later in life, when it appears and takes a seat in their hearts also.

Then perhaps they shall think of me, whom they love and smile, in spite of how badly it aches, because they know that I have felt it too. So that in many senses our pain may also bind us together in love, taking us back to where we belong, which is independent yet connected. Yes, indeed, our pain is a binding thing and a marrying together of souls and hearts and minds. It is good.

Life is too important for us not to be ourselves. This is the truth and for a long time I was running away from that awareness, but there it is and it's deeper than knowledge, or it is reality. The truth is that the longer you keep on pretending that everything is okay when it isn't, the longer you hold onto that view of hey, whatever, it's fine, "I'm just cruising", the more fully dead your insides become. Then the more increasingly hollow your actions become and the greater the distance between your true happiness in being and how you are choosing to live your life.

That is just how it is, a great big gaping chasm of love and loving, of which being real is part. Being real and attentive and allowing yourself the freedom to engage in true acts of living and loving kindness, are what matter. It is an interesting world which we live in and there are so many here with their own agendas, ideas, ideologies and more. It is absolutely essential that you find whatever is true in you and that you nurture it. For, that is what is given.

5 I HOLD YOUR SMILE IN MY HEART, QUIETLY

You rush me eagerly towards you
we are at breakneck speed
Silence dropping around us
and nearby the sounds mull

Happiness came dripping from a place of quietude. Really that was the surprise. It had not seemed possible that such a thing could have happened. That her eyes could have been opened in yet another randomly powerful, yet strangely gentle way. It may seem contradictory, but you see it was not the event itself that opened my eyes still more deeply, but rather a gaze. Her gaze.

It is quite a funny thing to be awakened by another person's gaze. I am sure you can imagine that feeling of their eyes creeping over your body. It is an interesting development, as it is quite a blessing.

You know that feeling when you sink your teeth into a Derida dried fig? You allow your tongue to dip deeply inside it, as your front teeth mount and tear at the outer flesh. All the while, that feeling of absolute satisfaction as your teeth grind on its seeds, tongue flitting back and forth along where bits of it have gotten stuck. Managing to uproot them, nibbling away, until there appears to be nothing left but that silent waiting thereafter. Waiting either for another fig, or to swallow the rest fully.

Well, say it's your last fig, right? So you do everything just like you did before, except that this time there is no waiting for the next one. This awareness adds such an element of beauty, uniqueness and fullness of expression to that experience. For you have no expectations as to what may or may not happen later on.

You have no sense of time, nor comparison, for that momentary enjoyment stands alone. It is neither beckoned inwards, nor given to reliance on any large or small subset of happenings, either subsequent or prior. Rather, it is whole. That is all there is. That is all that there shall ever be of that experience. Indeed, it actually does not matter if a similar experience occurs, because in actuality each one may look identical from outside, yet from within their differences are as brilliant as that of yellow and red.

The point is merely this, in happiness, in true and absolute joyful awareness; there is no continuum of experiences. It is not that you forget all that has come before, but, rather, that it is not like continuous time, where one experience is built upon that which precedes it and indeed compared with whatever may in any way or sense bear some sort of resemblance to it.

So that, within true happiness lies that beautiful sense of; this is different. This is an experience which is in the epicentre of all other experiences. Truly, it is that sort of awakening which her light has brought to me.

I am not yet certain which part of our encounter has done this. It has taken me greatly by surprise that someone of whom I knew so little could have such power. It is not my fault of course, life tangles us up in so many different people's happenings, we cannot be expected to be aware of everyone, all the time. Yet it does feel like I had to pass through certain levels of awareness in order to be able to share in this space.

The space is one of absolute silence. I cannot describe its depth, but it is absolutely everywhere in that moment. I find it strange, conceptually speaking, to communicate with a person who so directly answers my silence with her own. I don't know what it means. How can I? All that is certain is that there is a resonance far beyond words. It may just last forever.

If I were to say how and when I would of course have to call to mind that yoga class. I felt her eyes on my body during one posture, right before she let go and fell deeply into her own rhythm. It was nice to feel her eyes letting go of me like that, to feel that she was not hungry but merely liked to taste a little. I am finding that this is part of her way all of the time, which is nice.

The second thing that happened was afterwards, when she turned fully towards me and sat crossed legged on her mat. She was looking directly into my eyes. I liked that a lot. It felt like there was a space created between us, some sort of shared pocket in time.

This is not what drew me towards her though, not entirely at least. It was just this, that I went to ask a stupid question and without her doing anything in particular, I couldn't utter a word. She gives me pause. Beyond the silence which I am feeling that we share, she gives me pause. I feel that both of these things lend themselves to a bond predicated through very organic and natural acts and feelings.

For once I am aware of following my breath, instead of trying to capture, coerce or dictate that it do as I please. Which basically means that I have found my natural rhythm and have fully fallen into it.

She eases herself ever so gently into my life. Like how the leaves glide through the air in autumn, gathering in pockets which eventually form piles and piles of colourful pieces. Together and apart and absolutely whole.

I have this feeling like we were destined to meet. It may be the dreamer in me though, my mind laughs whenever my mouth intimates such things. How can you know! It says, ridiculing my hearts feelings and calling into question all that I cannot prove. Oh well.

It is not such a bad thing really, to have a mind which is filled with critique. It has to have something and I have spent my entire time alive following the whims of my heart and beckoning of my soul.

My mind is merely a tool with which to play with words. Slicing and dicing them up into succulent arrays of chunks, thickly sliced flesh of words, its liquid glimmering in the light as it sits still and heavy on the plate. Such things cannot last with you, for they are simply too heavy. Unless you might decide to become heavy like that too, mores the pity. Indeed, the liquid of your soul is not bare and free to glimmer as is, for it is enclosed a little and engaging in its work in silence and quietude and quite often, darkness.

Let us return to that which dances though, for some of which hold power and aid my meanderings through life with their content. Others, which are scraps, form piles of reminders, that too much is always better than too little. I have forgotten why I was once so afraid of love and loving, although it was most certainly through some sort of miscommunication. It seems that when people were behaving angrily or aggressively I assumed it was through a lack of love.

The truth is far grittier however; fear needs no lack of love to fester. There is no contradiction inherent in that person who is at once angry and aggressive and then a little later filled with love and tenderness. They run along parallel lines, until one is so underused that it falls into disrepair and eventually ruin. Which one does this is down to your choosing. It may change at any time, through those exact same means, but I digress.

I wanted to speak with you of her eyes. I do not

know how, but the light within them certainly contains the secrets to her power. We all have our own gifts and powers of course. We all also have our own light. It is not true that everyone can carry these things in such a way that they are evidenced through looking. Yet with her, it is so.

I cannot tell you of the ways in which this magical silence has moved me. I shall endeavour to try. It is a happy and joyful silence. Marked in between what happens today and then. It is carried between entire days, in moments, as in a full droplet of water which bursts effortlessly with its carriage. Emptying itself of its own contents, yet still emerging having lost nothing and merged with everything else to create something absolutely new and great. It is about each story not having an ending, because they never really began.

It is about touching of skin, feeling someone else's want and desire and answering it only with your own. All in such a way that nothing is given or taken exactly. Now that truly is a miracle, don't you think? I suppose it is something akin to the means through which all water is always returning to itself. Through seas, rains, ice and through us too. I suppose that these moments are earmarked in the book of life. That we are sat eternally facing one another on our yoga mats, with this effervescent silence which surrounds us, through which we speak.

I do not remember her accent, which is new too. I am particularly good at paying attention to such things. I have forgotten exactly what it was that we said, although I do remember some specifics. It feels so very far away and at once a part of us, whatever that means. In my dreams there used to be no talking. I liked them then because everything was understood without explanation or question at all.

Now it seems that my life has become silent and this in spite of words used and often in my dreaming there are so many words now, it is unreal. I am starting to feel like I have stepped into my own personal legend, which is why there are no questions and everything is absolutely understood.

I have a pain in both of my breasts just below the soft tissue. It comes every now and again and I know that eventually I shall have to attend the doctors. Every time that I am ill I think of death. Sometimes when I am not ill I think of it too, imagining how it might occur. It is always me having some sickness which brings me to the brink of death. I am quite certain it is breast cancer, although of course it could be anything.

Given the silence which surrounds me now, I have no fear of pain, discomfort, or death. Death for me is a beautiful thing and something I have experienced in part already, in many ways. It is true that in order to enjoy our dying and take it for the learning experience which it is, we must first live well. That means truthfully and wholly.

The silence I have shared with her certainly marks the beginning of that passage. While it is neither of greater nor lesser importance than what has come before, it certainly is the epicentre of all things now. That is a truth, another one. That life, this life, is at the epicentre of my being, rather than myself or my experiences, or even any of the people whom I love. Rather, life has gathered herself deep inside of all of these happenings and is dancing with me in mind, centre stage.

I wonder what other gifts she may be bringing with her. They say that all beings are a reflection of us. I do not believe in that exactly, yet it does feel as if true understanding is a form of mirroring. Yet the difference is that when we step away from the mirror, we do not keep that full reflection. We may choose to try, but inevitably, most of it is discarded, misplaced, reused and redefined.

Sometimes, we find ourselves also being redefined by it and by what it brings to light. Yet while the reflection in that mirror may remain the same, our insides, that which we come to understand said reflection through diversify, grow and evolve. We may never see the same person twice.

Do you know that when she gave me her notes that that was one of the deepest acts of intimacy – for me at least, that I have ever encountered? Perhaps it sounds like I am starved of intimacy, which is not at all true. Yet her handwriting, with all that determination, concentration and self, wound up into one, really introduced us. I felt that we were sharing in a way that is not done very often. I might be wrong, but my cheeks burned super red that whole tube ride home and I couldn't see a damned thing on the page!

The people around kept staring at me, with their shadowy senses of self. Who spends thirty minutes staring at the face of a person deeply enchanted by life? I can understand them glancing, but to be so very mindful is certainly a sign of depravity. Ones soul cannot be whole and lose itself entirely on another. It is simply impossible. How many people do we have in this world who are so lost yet through watching television have come to believe it is usual to spend so much of one's time and energy paying attention to what's outside?

It is true that it is not hard to train people in these ways. I have the feeling that any sense of cognitive dissonance the truth brings would be too great for many to accept the challenge. Many of us are caught up in this sense of "other" and "self", to such a great extent that we have imprisoned ourselves without knowing it. It seems to me that she has some light with which to make people aware that the lock is actually open and even if it wasn't, that they have the key themselves.

This is the quality of silence of which I have spoken. It is the kind of light that is beautiful, that creates space for others to look and see. It makes one aware of the shape and form of one's own soul, at the same time as enabling ones feelings and experiences to touch it, which may never have done so before.

This is quite something, given the sensitivity of

one's soul to newness. It is no small feat, that one might contain within themselves that capacity to reduce such a possibly traumatic, or severe and unsettling experience, into a gradual, sweet and gentle revelation within oneself towards this newness.

Furthermore, there is the question of not being reduced, nor changed nor challenged by these things. That the light which is beautiful and has created such space and awareness, does not infringe upon the natural self. I don't suppose there isn't a tree growing in any field that does not simply want the absolute pleasure of having full control over which of its branches grow and where. It is not a pleasant experience to have another come and sever ones choices. We none of us want that.

It is true that some of us get so used to this happening, that we start to partake in this experience against ourselves too. I suppose that this is partly where plastic surgery and re-constructive surgeries come in. I have yet to meet a person with either who was not wounded internally. Which is not to say that it is a bad choice necessarily, because we are most of us wounded somehow really! It is just that it is not necessarily a choice in all cases.

We think we are choosing, when we are not and the healthiest among us will admit that we were unhappy and be honest about our reasons. As soon as we admit to these things they lose their power over us and we get to celebrate all our choices, healing those wounds!

For me, it is not about being wounded, it is not even about what we need to help heal the wounds, it is just being aware of both these factors. Awareness allows full and complete healing, enabling us to share our experiences with one another, building bridges rather than mountains.

Regarding awareness too, when we look at how the relation between noise and space and, silence and space, is manifested in humanity, we can see the charms of both. It is not that one is superior at all of course; it is just that one is better suited to each concerned. For me, I would rather be bathed in silence which shares the light of awareness bringing all beauty to light, than its counterpart experience. I would rather have her come to me and sit across from me on our spread out mats. Even, perhaps, gazing into my eyes as she did.

Of course, it does not quite matter how a moment of truth manifests between two people. We could just as well be walking through a park at dawn, laughing and listening to the birds waking up. We could just as well be laying on the beach listening to the waves, or reading to each other. This dance of life requires little from us, in the sense of form and much in that greatly established sense of participation.

All questions being answered, I am glad of the opportunity of getting to know her. Or rather, for that expression implies a start, middle and an end. Rather, say that I delight in sharing this dance. Let the silence, light and the beauty which her gaze can bring, infuse my soul gathering here at the epicentre of my current existence for as long as it chooses to. For who would want more or less than that absolutely perfect expression of itself?

Yet too, I delight in the idea of an even greater deepening between us and I shall not deny that a short has already been written about things which I can't yet divulge. Some shades come to light sooner than others I guess.

Meanwhile, my only wish is that my presence illuminates somehow also. That us sharing, is a deepening and enriching process. That the beauty and truth of her own soul and self becomes more apparent in some of what I am "reflecting".

It would be nice to be able to gift something of that silence back. Although shared, there is always the question of separation of attention and hence, awareness's regarding what it is that is being shared! Quite a revelation from time to time, learning about our absolute differences in terms of perception. Also, about the lack in them, depending on the boundaries we have made around ourselves.

Depending on how open we are to the light of silence, as it creeps within us, deeply. Depending on how much we adore the noises our lives bring close to us. However, as for me, well, I am here and here I am, holding your smile in my heart, quietly.

LOST PHOTOGRAPHS

Through unfortunate events, never fully explained to me by my Mam, the suitcases containing nearly all of my childhood photos were lost years ago. Hundreds of images of me as a baby and child, gone forever.

When I discovered this, the loss of the past and sense of grief overwhelmed me. I just felt so deeply hurt and angered that so much of my life has either been sold (due to being in care and that prior to that I lived in many different houses) or lost without my consent. I am the only adult I know with no family home to go to and hardly any records of my past remain, beyond those belonging to the State or thankfully a few friends.

What helped me let go, was the kindness and effort of the people in Corofin Co. Clare particularly, who were eager to ease my pain through discovering images which were new to me! Particularly my Junior Infant School teacher Myra who eventually sent me images to my Grandfather's house in Waterford.

The mixture of joy, relief and compassion shared is what healed my anguish.

So, it struck me, that whenever life takes something material from us, invariably it replaces it with love, joy and some sort of kindness. At least that has been my experience when I've been able to step away from the pain.

I guess true healing will be when I'm able to wonder curiously what life will replace the next thing it takes, without any emotional reaction!

The images are broken into three sections spanning stages of my life. This first part is all I have of my early childhood and some older family images taken from my Grandmother's own biography.

It is a pleasure to share these rare and precious images with you!

Above: My Swiss-English maternal grandma Anna, marrying Bhupesh my granddad from Mumbai in 1963. Grandma remains my closest familial confidant and greatest support and most consistent inspiration. We are more friends than relatives to be honest and often howl with laughter while sharing stories and mischievous thoughts!

Below: Anna at a Swiss dinner party at the Oberoi Hotel in 1971.

Top: My maternal English Great Grandmother with my Mam Peshna, at the Sun-n-Sand Hotel in Juhu in 1967. Great Grandma used to call me 'chicken' and I adored her! We frequently exchanged letters during my

childhood which was a source of great comfort to me. She also gave my Mam Peshna the nickname 'Wiggy' because of the way she walked. **Middle:** My maternal Indian Grandmother Ba, with my Mam. Mam always spoke highly of Ba and I have vivid memories of how she used to soothe me after my nightmares

by assuring me of her presence and that she was taking care of us. **Bottom:** Mam in 1972 at the member's club, Breach Candy, which they frequented in Mumbai.

Top left: Mam and I **Top right**: Me aged 5 with my baby brother **Right**: Me aged 4, you can see my modelling skills shining through even back then.

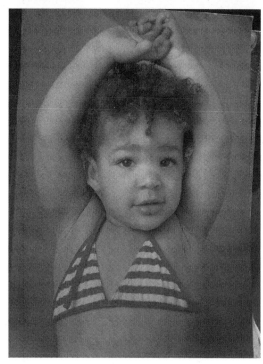

6 THE GIRL WHO OPENED DOORS

i can be your poster girl
Storing me up in your vision
of betterment, better than
i'll do that for you, and more.

It was after a hot sweaty ashtanga class that she received the call, from that voice. She had left a message which sent a ripple of exhilaration through the girl, so that she was ecstatic before even pressing redial. It was an easy call, among the easiest of her life. She was grinning and laughing throughout, sat at the table, drawing attention from receptionists and gym goers alike. Drawing gentle attention in the way that joyful occasions always do and joyful beings also.

She was going to be a star! Her moment had arrived, for finally they had seen and really recognised her potential. When the conversation finished with the girl's Cheshire like gleaming smile saying; "Yes, this is my passion, it's my dream" to which the voice answered "Well then, we can certainly help make your dream come true".

She felt like her heart had stopped and all the noise was silenced, for she could still hear it all, but it no longer mattered. Nothing in her life was to have the same quality in the time proceeding from that call.

It had made acting and her passion for acting, the epicentre of her life, of her true self. It made all else pale in comparison. It made her glad and happy; it gave her security and love. It gave her reasons beyond reasons and something that mattered beyond all else and we all need something like that in the end. It is just this which gives us the ability to say no with absolute conviction.

I miss the agency already. Yet in many ways it was saying yes to my dreams and the conviction that came with that, which led to my being able to say no – as hard and as often as I did. So that in many ways, what I am missing is real, because in the interim I have lost so many things. What it is that I am missing, are the irrelevant weighty things which I was carrying alongside me before I went onto their books.

I have lost much of that self. I do not miss her at all, there is lightness in my step and an ease with which I find myself stepping into my mood. I am exceedingly happy. For me, the missing is not a longing, it is an acknowledgement and in many senses a true celebration of what was wonderful and is past.

Sometimes the times in life when we are flowering are so fleeting and intense, that afterwards, one can't help but look at the petals and sigh, smilingly. It makes one full to the brim. It makes one thankful and the grace and gratefulness which floods through you, permeates your being, bringing more and more powerfully assertive actions to the fore. So that, somehow in the end it is you who is following your dreams and doing what you have always wanted to be doing.

Yet that is not what this tale is about. It is only about that girl, with that particular voice, carrying within it all the ways in which she could possibly lift you up. Steeped to the brim in beauty, a luscious lashing of light infused words flowed from her lips. She drove me out of the height of ignorance and into a state where I could not imagine anything other than my dreams coming true.

Of walking upon that red carpet, together with my love. There we will be, receiving the attention one needs and desires, having spent months wrapped up in the darkness of oneself. For that is exactly what acting is, the truth behind and within, the drama of the self. This, for me, is the journeying into a commune ancient and pure, with the awareness of those who have been there before and all who continue to go. It is a trek which is filled with love, anticipation and intense patience.

The girl opened the door within me to the safe passage back to my dreams. She held it with her words and her coaching. She held it with all of her being. Even as she keeps holding onto it now for others. Even as it's true that she will always be the first one who held it open for me also.

She was the first person outside of myself, who promised me that she could make my dreams come true. It feels like there is always going to be space where she once was there too, within our dreams which she held. Always space within her embracing that dream which we hold, nurturing and which somehow still continues to support and encourage, my very existence.

She held the door to my dream of belonging on Earth in her hands and pulled it open letting me enter within and I shall never forget that. When she left the space which remained could only be occupied by our fuelling those dreams and this capacity alone is such a gift. That she held open the door and made all these dreams mine and others so real, is a gift so highly sought after it cannot be valued highly enough.

She came into my life at a time when I was dreaming and trying desperately to make these things manifest and she taught me, that by believing for long enough, I was capable of making them real. So, it was not just a door to my dreams which she held, but that extra special door which exists between our dreaming and our ability to make our dreams into reality.

Still so, I shall reflect always on that moment, when she presented her voice and her guarantee, the first I had ever heard above and beyond my own. It is this that I will always carry within me, which I shall continue sharing with others. I am certain that there shall be others, other voices, other believers, others who encourage, facilitate and whose presence empowers simply through being there.

It does not in any way diminish her potency, or the power of what she said, for all things are additive. The good, gets carried along with you, into all of eternity, even as those which are bad, simply never stop dragging you down into forever on their terms alone. Yes, it is simply like that, as it has always been.

Life is pretty simple when you step out of it for a moment. Patterns emerge and you come to notice a particular rhythm to it, which is at once a soothing appeal to dance through life and also, a drum roll, with your own particular insistent beat, carrying on until the very end.

Long may you beat your own drum and longer still may others support your rhythm, appreciate your passion and support your every move. As for those who don't, well we are not all on the same journey, as my friend recently made me aware of and we are in no way given to demanding that those who are not part of ours, ought to credit us with any sort of awareness, belonging, or even acceptance. Such things are grand once we love and accept ourselves and our own journeys.

For then, we are free to celebrate together with those who truly celebrate us and also, to leave others to their own devices whenever they need that, without taking it personally, or feeling at all bereft. This sense of belonging to yourself is more beautiful than you can imagine and it is completely within all of our control, which is nice! The best things in life are free and often gentle, like how we are gifted our dreams, by naturally beautiful souls such as The Girl Who Opened Doors.

7 THE HINDRANCE

I want you to scream as I have done
Wrapping your soul's ears for fear
Their inner hollows may burst

She came to find me like she usually did. Even though I was now standing with my back towards her and my hands over my ears, with my eyes tightly squeezed shut. Even then she came. And she didn't just come either. She arrived screaming at me. Her voice heightened in pitch by the intensity of the absolute outrage which she was feeling... and time stretched itself out.

She came with all of her energy pulled out and extended over that taut line of her tonal intentions. I already understood more than I wanted to and my hands were attempting to ally my fears, to stop some aspect of the deepening awareness I had and was getting bombarded with, from perforating the bubble of my uncaring jubilant soul.

My soul was free at least. It was the only part of me which was, the only aspect which she could not get a hold of. Neither with her fingers, with their sharp short nails which were forced into my soft young flesh. Nor with her anger and pain, piercing me with its arrows at every possible chance.

So you see she could not get at my soul. I knew that from the time I read Michelle Wandor's book, given to me by her – funnily enough. I remember reading the story and understanding something deep beyond anything there was to be understood by merely reading and listening to the words. I understood their deeper meaning. I understood it then, as I understand it now and as I am about to share with you, my newest friend.

The story was a sad tale of a woman who seeks possession. Now, because she has decided that she wants to be possessed you see, because of this, her soul has to squish down deep inside of her body. It has to find some corner where it can hide, so that the other soul may take possession of her. That's the truth.

It was this book that helped save my soul. It was all the books I read, about religions, spirituality and love, with all their hope and lack thereof. It was the people I met and the experiences which we shared and it was the love my very same mother had given me when I was a baby.

That same mother who now shrieked and whose lips trembled so hard that spittle ran out of her mouth and down along their edges. How I hated the sight of the ugliness her anger portrayed, the thick scent of cigarettes hanging in the air around her. How I hated being alive to see such ugliness and more so, how I hated to feel such fear.

Her hand was heavy when it landed on my shoulder. And it had taken such a very long time to land as well. It had taken nearly forever and even then it took longer. The immense energy she put into it landing at the particular spot at that time, made the air move suddenly. It created something between a loud thud and a whispering sound. It all felt so strange.

My ears were trembling at the sensation and I had

the feeling that her anger fed hungrily and well on my fear.

This knowledge made me feel sick. Yet I wasn't in any position to be strong then, I didn't really know how. My child's mind that had been so well loved, was still in much confusion regarding where that tenderness had gone and I didn't really know how to respond to such brute force as was used.

As an adult now, I understand that too often those who have been de-clawed are taken and beaten by those who can't be. I think every kind of way of being is like a spirit that possesses a person's soul and that at that time, an angry spirit housed where my mum's heart used to be. It feels like she was in too much pain to see clearly and that hurting so deeply and lacking support and love, made her mad.

It's true that she was a beast of a woman, but normally only towards me. Perhaps at that time a sad spirit fed on her beautiful heart, as the angry one set fire to it over and over again, laughing through her laughter, as it ran in circles around the room, curdling milk and minds at once. Mostly mine, it has to be said.

The neighbours were long gone with their jubilation at having found a new queen bee to follow and praise and laugh with when told to and to admire and look up to and honour and obey until death do us part. The attending hearts had left and left her without their riches. Without the spotlight under which to simmer and burn. Without the adoration as balm to soothe the wounds of being alone and frightened and angry and sad. Without the balm of their love and adoration, of their acceptance without challenge.

This was the most important part for her mind was always challenging her. Her mind was always asking her why, telling her what to do and when, questioning all of her choices and making her scream inside like a child with no one there to hold her. The truth was that it felt as if she hadn't ever had them. So, as this is not yet her story, let us return to that scene.

Those people have all left us now. Everyone has been gone for at least an hour and in that hour darkness had descended like never before. Her hand was gripping my shoulder so tightly I yelped and she shouted;

"Well turn around then! What are you doing you stupid little girl hmm, you think you're being clever do you? C'mon look at me Johanna, please, just turn around for god's sakes. What's wrong with you? Why are you so scared of me?"

These cat and mouse games were always the worst. She would come closer with her alcohol infused breath burning hot against the back of my neck and cheeks. I would feel her spittle landing here and there and shudder, as bile rose inside me from pure disdain.

My throat was always raw those days and I was always grateful for some sort of feeling inside which I had created myself. It may have been from the force with which I thrust my fingers back my throat, the nails tearing at my softness, making the puke pink.

The disgust I felt then, in those times, hardly came out. If it did it would invariably prompt a smack. Perhaps across the face, with the backs of her fingers, or a shove against my arm. Sometimes, it would make an eyebrow raise, she loved to play with me and draw me out, making me as afraid as she could. She enjoyed making me tremble with fear.

Sometimes, I couldn't take it and I would break down into a shuddering, shaking torrent of tears, quaking from deep inside my body. She would usually either snarl, or laughing say;

"Well what is it now hey? AW! POOR YOU... look at you, you're so BADLY treated hmm... well maybe I should call social services hmm? Get you taken away? Wouldn't that be better Johanna."

All said with this thickly sarcastic lilt to it. All of her words were spoken down to me. I was already facing her now, well, if you could call it that. I found myself there, curled up, knees bent and in a squatting position with my hands wrapped around me tightly, or covering my face.

Whatever I did I tried not to look at her eyes, because she would react immediately, but sometimes the pain got the better of me, or the anger and I would either shout, or look at her with all of those intense feelings in my eyes. Yes. It was like that between us then.

It was like a hell from which there was no release and the circles which we went round and round in, saved us from ever risking feeling anything new and perhaps also more caustic. It was hard to love, hard to let go and get vulnerable. It was hard to hear things, hard to listen, hard to speak and understand. There was an absolute breakdown in communication and even now I dread going home for Christmas until I am actually there.

The fear, pain, anger and intense trauma of those hellish days have branded us, our minds and we are subject to different kinds of anxieties and fears now. I spoke with my mother a few days back, dear newest friend and her voice was all high pitched. I hate that we have these memories which are holding us back and I hate the anxieties, anguish and anger which they promote.

I wish I could forgive her pain and the pain which she caused me and I wish that she too could allow the past to stay there. I want for us to be okay again, for us to let go of those hardships and struggles. I want for our anxieties and fears to get well and for us to be able to love again.

On the phone earlier, she was so scared at the idea of Christmas, so worried perhaps I wouldn't come, or that my brother wouldn't. It could have been something to do with money, or it could just be that Ireland intellectually speaking is perpetuating a state of fear in this time of recession.

For me at least, the idea of home, breeds fears.

This is because what I did know then contained so much of that. When I see people getting excited at the known, I realise then how very wounded I am, not to be able to feel like that at the prospect of going home for Christmas, although I may want to and have moments when I am. It most certainly is mainly panic and fear, when I am moving towards those places, with those same people whom I associate with the many ways in which I have broken.

Funnily enough, although fear is spoken of broadly and widely, it is not something which the people actually feel as deeply as love for example. Emotions are very real in Ireland and we take strong likes and dislikes to individuals who are more intuitive and we stand by these. They are deeply understood and felt and hence they have earned their value in our lives and psyche. I grew up there and having moved away and gained a more objective perspective, it is absolutely clear to me that this is thus, at least among my people.

This is certainly true within the circles in which I move. The bonds and ties that people in Ireland have for one another are pure. The deeper understanding and acceptance of human nature, with all its foibles and then, the ability still to say no when necessary to those who could do harm to you, is divine.

When somebody is sick there is such compassion for that soul it is unreal. Everybody knows and understands inherently that all forms of mental and emotional sickness are caused by trauma and fear. The complexity of humans, the simplicity of the truth and the reality of every situation are embraced and understood without words being directly spoken.

I feel that this is the aspect of the culture that my mother can never understand. She thinks so much and so many of her thoughts are followed by direct speech and words which aren't at all poetic and sentences without any layering, that for her when people speak of fear, it means fear. She is immune to the cushioning effect of having grown up in a country where words are often used to connect things far deeper and much more important than anything that can ever be said.

Yet, I don't suppose that there are any excuses for her behaviour at all. I always make them and now have promised to never make any. I have asked her before why she beat me as a child and she said that it was a coping mechanism. That she was under extreme stress, finishing her degree, raising two children with hardly any cash, she had just lost the man she was in love with to a road accident and she used me as a means of getting rid of her stress.

Which is all well and good, when speaking of the aftermath of that accident and even when she was studying her degree. Yet this incident which I have shared with you dear friend, this happened two years hence. It happened when I was breaking down into my eating disorder. It happened after the stress had gone and she just kept on going. I feel strongly as I write this that she was afraid of loving again and that she had become a fully blown alcoholic at this time.

As you may know, alcoholics have two faces, one of a saint and the other of an approximation of Satan. Well, I was almost entirely privy to the latter and it happened not just because of the alcohol. It happened because the day after her drinking and all of that ugliness she had tried to paint onto me.

The day afterwards, whether she had to work or not, she had forgotten the most part of it. So that by the time she came home, tired and having spent all day thinking about her children's dinner perhaps, or school, or whatever. She would get home and I would be icy cold to the other side of her. This would make her angry and sad.

It must've been so hard for her, for a woman as loving and caring as she is, with such a soft delicate heart. To realise how badly she had hurt me and to see that actually in my inability to eat. To see her first born moving so very far away from her and not knowing what to do. It must've been super hard for her to have seen that and felt it and lived it.

You see for me, I was already numb. I mean I felt mostly pain, or nothing. I liked it better that way, I no longer trusted the world and had decided that I had had enough with loving people. It was too late for me now to love anyone ever again and I didn't care to anyway. I was tired of life, of moving and of being told to lie to people about who we were and what had happened to us.

I felt like I couldn't really make any friends without them being taken away from me. I felt like I wasn't allowed to love and I assumed it was punishment for having made the wrong decision as a child. I believed that I deserved to suffer. I gave up on life, living and loving and despaired of it all. The way that my mother was treating me just reiterated what I already felt I knew about the world and made it easier for me to say no. It made it easier for me to keep on saying no!

The thing was, I mean my friend, the most important thing is, that as soon as I moved away I realised that the world was different. There were things that I did, things which were strange and uncanny. Some things which perpetuated the ideas that her behaviour towards me had made manifest, as they remained unchallenged.

Yet, eventually, other people, with their separate reactions and ways of being, came and infiltrated my mind. They resonated with my heart so well, that I had to start moving towards them. I had to start letting go of all of that pain and anger, of all of that anguish and fear inside. I had to move towards the love and the light which they had shown me and be there with and for them. Not to mention, being there with and for myself also, as I came to discover much later on.

The darkness which my mother carries is still there. She wears it like a shield against the cold, stark reality of living her life alone for such a long time without intimacy or love. She wears it like a shawl to cover the wounds on her shoulders and body and to keep those around her from seeing her truth. She wears it as a baton, with which to draw out and beat herself and others too, if they are too bright for her, or if they come to close. She wears it as a torch, so that she may always walk in darkness and never find a way to be free of the burden of those things which she found in her past to be useful.

The things which she had to fight so hard for, even if they are causing her back to ache, her body to stumble, her eyesight to diminish. Still in her heart she is happiest when able to carry and find these things, when able to utilise and share these treasures with her deepest self.

Then she can feel good inside at her own independence and how she has always managed to survive "somehow". How no matter how hard it has gotten, she has always managed to be able to make do and carry on. How she has always been in charge, in control of herself and ready for whatever trials and tribulations came her way!

I no longer carry darkness. I dispose of it at every possible chance and I am always getting rid of things which are in excess. This includes thoughts and behaviours which do me and others no good and ways of being which aren't beneficial. I am always letting go and getting lighter and shining more.

I was born a child full of love and it was only in my teenage years when I grew so confused that I burned with anger. It was only when confused, tired and alone, that I fell so far from myself. So that through not seeing properly, I felt myself lost forever, as I was already aware of all of the possible ways in which I might get up, but I could not, nor did I want to.

In my case, life came in with all of its beauty and light and loving tenderness, challenging me to go with it and to realise that it was there still. In my case I only wanted to die because I did not remember what life is and felt that it was only pain and suffering. I believed with all my heart and soul that it was darkness and I lived under a constant cloud of fear.

In my case, it was life which chose me and I who was ever so grateful, even when I didn't fully believe in its beauty and power. Even when I didn't fully understand the truth in what it meant, or why it kept choosing me. Still I wept happily and rejoiced.

It was through life's constantly choosing me and my constantly being grateful to and for life, that I changed and grew. It was through all of these people and experiences and my understanding of how miraculous they all were especially, in the context of the hell which I knew could exist, that I was able to finally be myself, to rejoice in that self and love that self for always.

The thing is too that during those times, I also slammed doors; I wandered deeply into my own depths and used things to hurt her too. I used my own self destruction as a force through which to cause her harm. I don't believe in right and wrong, I feel that these are judgements born of utter ignorance. I hurt her as much and hard and often as I could and the only reason I was seen as the victim in that situation is because of my age.

I agree that I didn't start things, but we were in effect both part of their beginnings and for so many reasons we both became entangled in a bitter battle. I would use all of my money to buy food and then spend hours puking it up.

It even got to the stage where I was afraid to leave my room and draw attention to myself so I could get sick into plastic bags and store these under my bed. It was only ever until I could manage to actually throw them out, but how horrendous is that? Now, looking back I can feel my sense of self disgust and disdain and also how my actions helped fuel, facilitate and fan the flames of my mother's desperation.

Yet, neither of us were actually victims if you ask me. We both chose our actions and continued to carry them out. The truth is that all either and both of us ever wanted was love and that was what we were fighting for. The truth is that had either of us been more able to see that, that the other person was only ever demanding love, then things wouldn't have escalated as they did.

However, I would not give up that experience of darkness for anything now, because nothing surprises me and hence I am grateful that those around me feel free to tell me about their secrets. Others around me feel good and safe and willing to tell me whatever they have hidden from people, because they can feel that I won't judge them and that is the greatest gift I've been given from all my pain, being here for others.

Of course, that comes after being here for myself though! I also hurt myself in order to let go of the feelings of anger and deep loneliness and because of my own confusion at myself. It happened because I was seeking some sort of relief; probably the same reason mother drank so much to be honest. We were two innocents in lots of pain and it was such an intensely difficult situation I cannot tell you. Let us return to the initial story now though.

It has evolved so that now when she comes to find me, I am always standing straight and looking at her. So when she comes to find me, I am always with a look of joy and light and love in my eyes, channelling all of those people I've met, loved and shared with.

I stand for all of those experiences I have come to celebrate and share and celebrate with others. I stand for all of those times when I have fallen into darkness, not in the same shade perhaps as hers, but made of that same material and I have torn it up and thrown it off and left it somewhere sacred to remove its fear and unknowing.

So that now when she comes for me, I am absolutely ready and armed to the teeth with a smile and a hug and oh so much love and truth and warmth for my mother. For the woman who has left herself behind to come and find me once more.

So that the darkness with which we once played, might know that regardless of whether she carries it with her, or still needs it somehow, she no longer works with or for it. So that now when she comes to find me, she is coming from the light in her heart, with light for her hearts child.

So that now when she comes to find me, she reaches her hand in towards my face in tenderness and says;

"Johanna darling, do you want some more brussel sprouts?"

I smile at her shyly. The air of a young girl of perhaps fifteen about me and I say;

"Yes please mum."

My brother stretches and smiles, my Grandmother beginning another rant with those beautifully blue eyes of hers, surrounded by such beautiful creases borne of experiencing life. So that now when she comes to find me, I am here, in love and surrounded by love and we are all well and good and it is Christmas and we are all here and all together, at last.

This experience of the perfect Christmas actually happened the year after I wrote this story. It began with me feeling ill and she did start at me when I arrived into the sitting room. I had been dreading this, but instead of hiding from it I turned to her looking into her eyes said;

"No Mam, you are not allowed to bully me anymore."

It was this that led to the beginning of something new, due to the death of The Hindrance.

8 THE LOSS OF SPACE

Like That
The darkness protruded
Through my mouth
A wail escaping
Telling of nothingness…

The anger came from nowhere, yet it was everywhere all at once. She saw it in the faces of the people whom she met at the shops. Lips taut, eyes narrowed, a bleak perception of reality written all over their stance, it was an appalling state of affairs.

She breathed in sharply, deterring the inevitable fire which had begun rising from deeply within her. It came from her stomach, right up out of the depths of her belly and it fed all of her instincts to bite.

She was angry too now and she liked it. She liked it better than that soft eager wanting to please everybody which had assailed her for so many years hence. It was a different sense of being and it made her stronger. She felt taller and it gave her a strength she didn't remember having before. Yes, this was good, yes, she was much better.

That moment came and went in a flash. Then she was home again and she turned around to her mother. In this moment, she was disgusted at herself. It struck her as undeniably ugly to employ bestial emotions such as anger and begin to adapt to them. She didn't want such ugliness to adorn her character, she had never wanted that and yet somehow here she was, growling.

She had always only ever wanted to be beautiful. She craved being so good inside that she became one of the most beautiful women the planet had ever known! She hadn't told anyone of course, given her awareness of her own ugliness and the amplitude with which she felt her own vulgarity. She couldn't imagine ever expecting anything but laughter upon returning said visions upon her friends and family. They would laugh at her, she shuddered, coming back to the reality which had gripped her shoulders roughly.

Spluttering on her tea she heard the last of her mother's curt words. Flushing red, she realised that she had been mocking her for quite some time and that all her mum's friend's were laughing too. That hurt.

It rippled like a fire in a barn filled with hay. The roof of her thoughts collapsing in upon themselves. Inside of her was so hot, so very hot, she couldn't think. She couldn't feel properly either, it ached so badly. Yet still the fire was spreading. She tried to enunciate her words, but her mouth was dry, she couldn't swallow anymore and nothing was working.

The fire had taken her soul. It had taken her breathing. There was even no space for her voice. Her insides felt dark and filled with this heavy toxicity. As she spluttered in pain, mucus fled out of her nostrils, catching on people's clothes around her. They made faces which matched how she was feeling and it hurt. Everything did, inside and out, there was no escape.

There were thick salty tears and her chest shuddered with such great intensity that she couldn't help but moan loudly. For a moment afterwards there was silence. She had cracked through their intensity, but only for now. Then the heat caught on again and like a strong wind fanning flames, the people present began to howl. The intensity of their laughter was fierce and they really were all laughing at her.

She felt appalling, she was appalled. She wanted for the flames to reach up from inside of her stomach and swallow her whole. She wanted fumes to pour from her nose, funnelling through her nostrils and diminish this awful crowd to a human milieu of spluttering images, cloaked in the deepest, darkest, thickest smoke. She wanted that smoke to come from the utter destruction of her own being and for them all to be horrified within that experience.

Instead, it was she who moved her feet and ran away. Running into her room and slamming the door on the echoing of their toxicity, she sobbed. Sliding to the floor, the sobbing emerged in the absence of smoke, yet still her innards had melted. Crumbling from within, she fell; from somewhere deep within her, fires still rose, hidden in the disparity between her own destruction and apparently being together. It was a mess.

She began sobbing, but had stopped, to listen to their laughter. Every word was clear too, supported by the sound of her hard sharp breath rupturing. It came to her then between tears, that from now, it was going to be different and it would never be the same again.

In that moment, she decided it was time to take control. That anger which burned made her look deeply inside herself, to find the tools necessary to fight her way out of this heat which she hated. She hated it! Yes! Each finger curled tightly into the fists, nails biting into the palm. This was rage and as there was nobody there to help, she would just have to help herself.

It came to her then, what to do. It was time to use the powers she had found. To start standing up for herself.

There would be no more running. Nobody was anywhere she went to run to anyway, not even herself.

She had liked that sense of belonging, when the fierceness had come, making her breathe fire. It had made her feel glow, just then, how brightly she raged, feeling stronger than ever before. In that moment, it had become her truth and her only reality. Finally all her pain had meaning, as it could finally be used.

Days later she came for her once more. As usual, there was some obnoxious premise, perhaps justified until it took that malicious vindictive tone. Her mother's tongue produced a tone which would curdle even angels blood when it so desired and her daughter was certainly not immune. Indeed, given her new skill set, she did not bow her head as usual, nor was she afraid any longer, for she had already died.

Looked towards her mother, made the fire inside her spark. The flames licked her inside and her eyes glowed with anger and hatred. This was her new place of power. Somehow too, this it made all the difference.

The folk who usually surrounded her mother, had gathered as usual in the kitchen, it was dinner time and the games were about to begin. They all wore these looks of amusement and expectation. They were all so ready for the action, would it be the same as yesterday? Or perhaps, even better this time?

Darkness fell abruptly. The shadows which the sun had cast on the inner wall of the kitchen lengthened, extending themselves downwards and across. The light had lost its' power. It was time to play.

"So, there you go my beautiful child, the food which you may or may not eat!"

"Thanks Mam."

"Ha! Don't forget to clean the toilet bowl after you puke hey! God forbid you leave any remains there for us to see."

They cackled, bellowing laughter escaping their

lips before the sentence had even finished. I was waiting for my moment and it had come. Rising slowly in my chair, shaking, I caused the first ever pause of power.

"Why do you have to be such a god damn bitch about it hey? I'm your daughter for fucks sake AND I'm SICK... don't you understand that? Huh? Don't you think that perhaps it's a little normal that after the life I've had I might be affected? Fuck you! Eat it your god damn self!"

At no point did I stop looking at her. The satisfaction felt as the colour drained from her face was truly incredible. It had been years since I had felt this good. It felt so wonderful to me, to finally be free from fear and shame. To actually be able to respond to her without crying.

Nobody was laughing when I left the kitchen table that evening. Nobody was laughing and I hadn't eaten a bite and I felt great. I understood absolutely my own power in that moment. The power to externalise the pain. The power to turn all that had been inverted for years, outwards, onto their source. How dare she treat me like that! Who did she think that she was? Hey? Bitch!

After that the fighting began in earnest, but oh my wasn't it beautiful. There were her nightly drunken ventures into my room to drag me out by the hair. At other times, the door would slam open, I knew she was coming for me from the moment I heard the front door. Yet, knowing that, I still begged all my angels to prevent her from entering my room. I still pushed my entire body back against the wall and dragging the covers towards me, tried so hard to disappear.

Nothing I did could stop her and she would slam the door open cackling loudly, the alcohol fumes thickly scented with nicotine. How I hated that smell! Eventually, following a dark speech she would lie with her full weight on top of me, whispering vicious and poisonous words into my ear.

I would cry and she would call me pathetic. I

could hardly breathe it hurt so badly. I tried holding my breath but then she would enjoy poking me with her sharp fingernails. Everything I did felt bad. I felt so, so ugly and alone and everything hurt.

This is how it used to be, until that fire started and then somehow, it was all good. The power which she held over me had diminished and I no longer felt like a victim. Nearly everything she did fed my anger; I used her words while exercising. I would skip rope for hours, sometimes whipping my own arms by mistake and laughing, as she did. I would sit behind the door with my back to it to stop people entering and would use the blade to source blood from deep beneath my skin. It felt good, being angry then, just like she was. It felt like home.

Even those trips when she came into my room drunk, became something else pretty shortly afterwards. It was almost as if she would fling open my door, standing there shouting as if to see who it was living there. She didn't have that same power as before and she never regained that space in my life again. She lost the honour then too also, as someone in my life as someone whom I looked up to and respected.

It was then that I started reflecting on how she had been behaving towards me down through the years. So that I found myself starting to ridicule her. Inwardly and outwardly, I ridiculed her and the corners of my lips curled upon her entrance. Always having been quite communicative about the ugliness of life, she was not at all hesitant to point this out. It was always her voice trying to make me feel bad about myself and my decisions.

This was done through trying to manipulate me into feeling bad about myself. It was an academic slight, absolutely irrelevant to one who already understands that such behaviours come from the desire to control. Indeed, once that awareness is there, all that it does is to alienate that individual from the rest of us.

My mind would be reacting to her words thinking,

are you really so dumb as to believe that your opinion matters more than how you are behaving? Seriously, you can say whatever you want to me, in whatever tone of voice you choose. Don't you know that, when I walk away and your words haven't sewn their seeds inside of me, I shall be free. I shall remain free also when in your presence, do you know that? You can't hurt me anymore Mam.

Well, let me tell you, disregarding my anger at that time for the moment, which was another trap actually. So, let us look at the ways in which you were expressing your intent to trap. Your words, your tone of voice, how you kept trying to make me believe that you were superior. All of these things are just illuminating your own weaknesses. It is just showing me that you are too busy trying to trap me, to actually be free. That is all that I am seeing, for that is the one true reality.

Honestly, when I became empowered by the fire which raged within me, I saw you then, with disdain. I understood immediately the fallacy of your attempts to entrap me and it made me freer than I could ever have imagined being.

Now, I do not recommend being angry for the sake of it. It is not that at all, merely that the rage elevated me at last to a place where I could see where I was and why. I could finally see who you were, how you had become and what you were doing to me.

That is all. The thing is with these tools though, that if we are unaware of the ways that they work, we may get used by them. That is because these forces are all quite strong. When used in the right circumstances, with the right sorts of intentions, they can attribute us with all the power we need.

Having said that however, I am now in the grips of a fire following a break up in a relationship. While I know that it wasn't the one for me and am happy to be out of it, it is more complex than that. It becomes more complicated because the ways in which we fall, are often into spaces which we may have left behind, but perhaps we didn't clean them effectively enough. It is true that life shares similar tests and lessons with us until we have learnt from each.

Part of my lesson this time is to address my anger, which was an expression of the deepest hurt which I felt. It is through these writings that I am addressing all I have chosen not to address until now, so that I may move onwards. So that my slate may be cleaned and I may be able to progress even further and more and more deeply into life herself. This is the plan and more than that, this is the path which I am walking.

I am not certain, but it's probable that it's the same path upon which all of my true friends tread. We are all walking together towards the absolute freedom of ourselves and we will all get there in increments. It is through sharing these experiences that we will come to understand our own. I am so grateful to all the stories and their tellers in my life. Even the ones that I have chosen to leave behind, because you are too heavy for me to carry without negating my own needs.

The anger, yes, the anger certainly has its place. It is a very good thing to have it as a resource to call upon. It is a greatly empowering and insightful tool. Yet, it must be left alone more often than it is employed and one must reach a space where it is never employed as it has become redundant. I have come to understand that the power in most of these tools is not in their use as many people may believe, but rather in their being left behind. In their being kept within the spaces of our souls, hearts, minds and bodies, to be used when we choose to, only.

Indeed, the greatest gift these tools give is our understanding where they come from, how to use them and when, if at all. This is their greatest gift to us; our knowledge of their existence within our repertoire can give us such strength. Why not use the tools you have to enable rather than disable you?

Yet I digress, the loss of space which another takes, becomes exactly the one which you fill. Remind yourself of that sometimes, for we have so many more places to go where that knowledge is necessary for us to remember. If we forget we may find it unbearable and perhaps never be able to return from The Loss of Space.

9 WANTED

And the crispness with which you saturate my mind
eases herself across all manner
of departures, flaking like
candlewax and the intensity of
changing between coming and being

I can't believe the effect that that sentence had on me;
    "I want to see you."

    I responded immediately and it was only afterwards when I reread that message that I found myself later, stood on the tube, hurting. Somehow, I had misinterpreted your actions to mean that you didn't want to see me. That was such a hard truth to hear back, most people don't see beyond what I tell them to. Or at least, they hardly open their mouths to tell me anyway. Gosh. What a wake-up call.

    I feel like you can see all of me. I don't know if that makes it better or worse, that you may be out fucking someone else right now. To be honest, I don't know if I can handle meeting up with you now, knowing how I feel about you. I think it may be best that we don't meet again. It would hurt too badly, you know, knowing that you would be having all of these men or women, loving you. It hurts me to think of it. It hurts.

So now I know how it feels to be falling in love and I don't know if I like it. Especially, given you may not be feeling the same way. I mean, I am supposing that you don't if you did, how could you go with all of those other people? I don't think that that would be possible for you. I really don't. So, I must take the initiative and take a step back.

It's not good for me, for my heart to be crushed by such awareness. I cannot handle it. I know that. It would crush me alive. How could I breathe babe? Knowing how you've enjoyed those others? I don't know how! It would be even worse, knowing that you've enjoyed them. It is not just about flesh, it has to do with souls, with spirits and minds.

I guess that we could meet, perhaps once or twice; I mean it is during the daytime anyway. I know you don't want to date me, because you chose to only invite me for lunch! No, I can't come! How can I! It is terrible! In fact it's the worst yet! Why do I always keep falling for all of these absolutely impossible women? It's so awful! My heart is literally burning! How gross. I feel so very vulgar.

Well. Maybe if I lose a stone I might feel better! Yes! I think that if I manage to lose a little weight that might be good for me. I think that if I manage to lose enough, I might forget about this pain in my heart altogether. That sounds like a good plan to me, to be totally honest.

If things don't work out that way, I might fall into a coma and die. I wonder if that's still considered romantic by other people? To die because of unrequited love! Well, I hardly care anyway. Also, I can't sleep and it's truly annoying me! I keep seeing your face flashing in front of me and I don't know why! I have done everything humanly possible to extract it from my brain.

I realise now that I've made an awful mistake, you

should never allow yourself to fall in love with somebody. At least, not until you know that they love you back. It's so terrible! What am I to do with myself now? She doesn't want me at all! I know it! She says that she wants to meet me, but what does it mean? A lunch. How horrid! To be relegated to the side lines. I hate it!

When will somebody fall as deeply in love with me, as I am with them? When will they make me their one, just as I make them mine? When will they want nothing more than to be with me always? I don't get it! How can I always be falling in love, yet they really don't reciprocate it at all. What am I? Who am I? Why can't you just love me as much as I love you? Is it really so hard to find your other half! Why! Why is it so hard! I don't understand, truly. I give up.

I know how it is now. The universe has decided that I should be alone. Alone. Alone. Alone. Always falling in love too! Which is even worse! I am like the world's biggest fool. How horrible! I want to die. I need to return to the light. To that place where I'm completely understood, accepted and loved. Thoroughly and utterly. Oh, how I hate this waiting.

Well. When I was younger I got down to around seven stone. I am sure that I can manage to do that again. That will be nice for me. To have something to do. To take my mind off all of this unreciprocated loving. I make myself sick, with the level of rejection which I am getting all the time. On all fronts. Gosh, I do hope that my university results are good! Can you imagine if not! That would truly be the death of me!

It hurts so badly right now! I wonder how long it's going to take to pass. It needs to go as soon as possible really. I can't be having this feeling forever. I know that I won't. Why does my heart feel so much so damn quickly! I hate it! I want to disappear! What's wrong with me! Why must I feel so much! Why must I share it!

If I hadn't have written her that text, if I hadn't have sent

77

her that stupid short story! It's so awful! I hate it all! Why must I be a writer? What good is talent when you can't find someone special to love you and appreciate it?

It's so awful. I thought that there was a reason for me living, beyond my own self gratification. I thought that I has some reason for being, but now I question that. What is the use of me, when there's nobody appropriate to love me? To believe in me? To want me enough that I become more than everyone else to them. I need that, because at the moment I am barely surviving.

So, after quite a lot of tears, I have made my decision. I am letting her go. That's just what I have to do for my own inner peace and tranquillity. You obviously do not care as much about me as I do about you. The simple fact that you are going on dates this weekend shows me that. Also, you already knew how I felt about you. You were the one who brought that about. So, I must take full responsibility for my heart. I must enable it to heal and to be free to love others.

So, as we have decided to keep our coffee meeting spontaneous, this automatically gives me the freedom not to contact you about it. Which is exactly what I am planning to do. There is simply no reason for me to hold onto your hand, when you so clearly want to hold so many others. It is a shame, actually. Yes, but it hurts me and I have too much to get done, to enable you hurting my heart. It is not good enough.

Perhaps, I shall also tell you that. Tomorrow, via text messages I shall stop this carry on before it goes any farther. I do not need anyone else to injure my heart, thanks very much! Ha! What do you think? I would actually accept second best? I don't think so.

It was very sweet of you to come to see me at the bar that night, it was awesome seeing you. However, I suppose that I read a little too much into it, as you don't want to date me! Perhaps you are dating men now, I do not know that. Nor do I wish to know. It is none of my business. We are hardly even friends, besides, if I move away now then there is a great chance of my healing quickly and finding someone new.

The longer I hold onto you, that idea has longer to fester and grow. Which is rather a shame. I need to sever that part of you which has gotten attached to me. I need to cut that chord as soon as possible, because I do not want to drown with your face in my mind. No way!

So tomorrow, at some point, I shall text you. Something quite sweet and short. Perhaps about freedom and love. I shall tell you that I already like you too much. That the very idea of you being with others, of you touching them and then you, hurts me.

Given that that is something which you shall be filling your summer with and perhaps even beyond, I feel that it is best that we cease all communication. Thank you for your time, I really enjoyed our exchange, but I also hope that I forget about you as soon as possible, so that I may move on!

So, there you see, is my process! Some parts miserable and filled to the brim, moving on towards our complete and utter freedom! I don't want to impose myself upon anyone. To be relegated to a lunch date is ridiculous and awful! I am one to be celebrated. I do not feel that you can offer me that now, for whatever reason. Indeed I shall write to you right now. I feel that that is best. End Rant.

10 YOURS, AFTER MINE

She came for a moment as a coating of dew does in the morning
in a world that has not yet woken up and as it is awakening
she is there glistening until suddenly she's gone.
Sometimes though, the beauty in natural occurrences are that
they find their own rhythm and it's up to you whether you wish
to be present or not.

YOURS

I want to write you into my being, into my bones as you say and I want for you to stay there always. I am aware that I might hurt you and that has scared me before. It still affects me now, but in different ways. Such as, the sense that I will love you even more fully and even more unreservedly, because of the feeling that nothing can hold me back.

I am aware, that there shall be times, when inadvertently, somehow and in ways which I do not mean, nor want, nor would I ever, that at times, sometimes, I will cause you pain. This has come to light now because of how I have hurt you before, just simply through being me and I am very sorry. It makes me so sad. I know also, that there are things which you shall do, which shall hurt me too, even as they did that time and I am sorry for that also.

Yes.

I want for you to come to me, gently and placing your hand in mine, enable me to rest by your side. I want you to let me hold you, kiss you and love you truly. I want you to know how deeply connected we are and how great that that makes me feel. I want you to realise that I need you in my life, as you are, as beautiful, angelic, sweet, pretty and fragile yet strong, as you are. I want to tell you the truth. I want us to be true. I want that.

You see the thing that my friend was right about, is that I was concentrating on how you were making me feel. It was all about what you were doing to me and how that was affecting me, rather than my affect on you and your heart. He was right, but not before I realised that I should not be following him, for he is great to listen to, but really, I can only ever follow my own heart.

This is a new understanding of truth. I have spent forever asking for peoples help. Perhaps, twice as long wanting to be led and now I am here, because you left me and broke my heart. It was burning so deeply that I had to let go, forcing myself to understand, that I could not follow these people, nor their advice. I could not pretend to be happy with entrusting them with our lives. The time has come to be making all my own decisions!

I feel like I am here to protect your heart. Perhaps even to save you and you are also here to save me. People keep on telling me that that's fucked up, but if love isn't about repairing what's broken and facing up to the challenges life brings, then why are we here? As far as I can tell, all those people who don't believe in love are broken and sad, lost and alone and trying, always trying to find some other way to be, some better reasons to hang on, except there aren't any. There is always only love, that, or your avoidance of it.

The truth is that all of those whom I have been listening to, don't have any of the kind experience of true love, which I was hoping for. Yet, there I was following them all, simply because they are in relationships. The thing is though, that they are with people whom are not their soul mates. They are with people who they have chosen in safety, so that they wouldn't break their heart. They have selected people in their comfort zones and that is exactly where they are dying right now.

You know what I love? Soppy songs about true love and black & white films about that as well. I know that love is something that breaks you and that it keeps on breaking you in all of these little ways and that is what I am drawn to in you. The constantly breaking and your essence and soul, which you share in your writing.

That is what I will always love in you too. I want you to hold me because you can understand what it is to be broken and to keep on breaking. I want that both of our breaking helps us stay together, all of those little pieces of us, becoming shards of our happiness.

I am aware that you touch the same darkness as I and also feel the connections we foster through shared pains and our history. The thing is that we have yet to meet in person though and I want that as soon as possible. Right now, it feels like it is taking far too long, we are only communicating via phone and internet and I can feel you. My intuitions about you are getting stronger, yet I feel helpless because I cannot hold your hand, or even kiss your cheek!

It hurt so much when you pulled away from me, my heart burned for real. I felt it when you felt me unfollow you on Instagram, it burned, it hurt so badly hey? Then when you got back to me, my heart felt so good and there was so much love that came out you cannot imagine.

I do not want for you to hurt yourself any more. I want to love you better, I want to hold your icky. I want to hold your icky and lick it and suck out all the pus. I want that, I want to help your poison to emerge from your sores and to place my lips on yours, for you to taste my tongue and realise that it's all okay.

I want for my softness to make you softer and for your softness to make mine gentler also. I want to belong within your fingers and allow your hands to hold mine. I want for us to dance together to the beat of that music which is in your soul. I want for us to dance and for our dancing to be more real than any other kind either of us has ever done! I want that to be because you and I, we belong in each other's arms. We were born to belong.

I want you to forget all that came before, even for a moment, because it doesn't matter anymore now, I want that. I want for things not to be perfect, for we are both bruised and breaking and that is okay also. I want to sit with you and look into your eyes and for that to be enough.

I want to wake in the morning to the sound of your breath and how you are breathing and be able to gently stroke the hair away from your face. I want to be able to hold you closer. I want to be able to watch as your chest rises and falls and to allow that to touch me from deeply inside. I want us. I want us. I want us.

I want for you to get back in touch with me and for that to feel absolutely great. I want to eat you out, to taste how your pussy tastes. I want to feel your thighs as they open to me. I want for your wetness to make me wet and for us together to keep getting wetter and wetter. I want us dripping, I want us new, fresh and clean, through being so very, very, dirty. I want for us to be. I want.

I want for our stories to always be intertwined. For you to sleep with your head on my chest, sometimes waking to your lips around my nipples might be nice. Seeing your face and it taking my breath away might be better. How easily we fall, how fully, how well we do it, how wholly. There is nobody else that will do. There is nobody else. There is no other kind of you.

I don't want you to need to talk to them anymore. I don't want you to want them at all. I just want for you to want me, the same way that I want you. I want for you to realise that I am yours. That we can get to be each others.

I want for our feelings to take over completely and for nothing to be impossible, because that's exactly how it is with feelings. I want for you and I, to be very much together. I want for us to play, run, hide and seek each other through every single method imaginable. I don't want anyone else and I am going to let all else go.

You know how I am now and when I am falling, there is only you, this is my heart. I am here. I am yours. I am bereft without you. I cannot live without you and I will not. You are my everything, my one, my only, my all. You are the sounds I am making when I am falling over and somebody catches me. You are the taste of sweet smoothies on my tongue. You are the way that I do not doubt our love, at all. You are mine, even as I am yours. For you are making it so. You have opened me up to your heart and I am totally here and ready and there is no reason for anything else to happen.

Now we just are ourselves and guess what? Everything escalates quickly. It just does, because that is what love does. It makes our hearts strong, it takes away the power of our minds and compels us to be together forever, to touch, feel and taste each other only, until no one else exists.

So that if this is love, really truly this is love, then that is what will happen naturally. We will only feel together within one another. We will only always be the one that the other was looking for. We only ever exist because of each other and that is always all that really matters. Of course, we shall continue with everything else that we are doing. Yes, we shall keep approaching life, living and being with others, but the truth is, that we are with each other first and we are loving one another together like this for always. We are forever and forever and this is all we are.

We belong with each other, we always have and

always will. The pain when we separate makes me question these things. Also, it is the beauty that your face, being, writing, your soul, pain and joy bring to my life. I mean really, I have been very lucky up until now, because of course, I have met so many people and done so many wonderful things. The only trouble is that I have not yet been ready to touch another soul with my own, without actually pushing them away because they couldn't just take it. Or perhaps, it was I that couldn't.

I feel that you are the same, somehow we have been pushing, yet how we push totally suits me. It is the sound of the summer of our hearts flourishing. It is the sounds of bells in a church, where everyone is happy to be celebrating our union. It is the realisations which we bring each other towards, in order to place the pains which we cannot yet reach, express in words, or even trust ourselves to, because they are just too heavy and dark.

Sometimes, I think that even if we could be honest with ourselves, it is hard to accept that it's not our stories which keep us separate from others. It is not, actually, the small things are what we find hard. That we might hurt one another, even that we might not want to. Getting over the realisation that we can hurt one another, is the hardest I think. Yet, it is what we do, just on occasion of our being alive, for we must be brave and it is better than trying to avoid life altogether. It is better loving, than trying to avoid it through fear of pain.

Today I was in the tube, this woman got on and I thought it was you and then I couldn't stop listening to your song. I had stopped listening to it as I didn't want to think of you and allow my heart to start burning as it did when we split up.

I had to go into my exam like that, after we had broken up, with my heart burning a hole right through my being. I had to do that. I had to go into that room with that fire burning and use my mind, even though I felt like I was going to die. Even though, I felt like I could not breathe. Even though I was burning so slowly, with this absolutely excruciating pain, I could do nothing to stop it, that was the worst part. I had to sit there writing for my exam, in absolute agony. It was horrific.

I do not know why I felt it so strongly, but perhaps I am sort of psychic. It might just be that I am the kind who can feel things from and about other people, an empath. This makes sense to me, that I am more connected than I thought I was and that connection lies beyond physical constraints.

I think that maybe I can feel you when you and I are connected because I will allow myself to do that. I reckon too though, that when I am with the wrong sorts of people, when I am surrounded by those whom I am aware are more restricted in their minds, that changes me and the way through which I am communicating.

I feel myself growing more and more aware that I do not want to talk, let alone share my innermost secrets with these people. It can sometimes become overwhelming to the point of extreme shyness and avoidance, until I can leave. Being socially awkward is no fun!

I have understood that I love people with all of my heart and that those whose minds will not allow them to love me back as freely, are missing out, because I love really, really well. I love without restraint. I love in all honesty and bare my soul and sometimes, my soul catches fire and the ashes which the fire creates, leads to more.

These cinders are what nurture when new loves grow and also what replenishes areas made barren by all of those older loves. Yet still in the wake of those, there is but grey ash and if I am to look upon those for too long, I might forget what is about to happen and instead stay focused on how very dull they are, their musty smell and how awful it feels. I might just do that.

At times, it is so easy to forget what lies beneath things. I live so fully in the moment that sometimes, I do forget to dig deeper. This can be beneficial because you can reap rewards from not judging people and also learn all kinds of lessons too.

Like with you, with you I did not hesitate for even a moment. There was absolutely no sense of uncertainty or despair and incredibly, what has occurred between us is a deepening of our trust, love and understanding. This is of both us and each other.

Before your arrival I was so scared that I might never be able to share my darkness with others. Now, I am so grateful that I can tell you almost anything and you will be so supportive and good with it. We have a very good connection in this sense then, although I do wonder about your responses when I tell you positive stories. I feel sometimes that these push you away and I wonder if that shall last?

What I wanted to say to you, before we physically meet is, that I am very happy with our journey. You have awakened in me this thirst for life, unlike that which I could have felt otherwise and I cannot tell you how refreshing is! It feels like new life. I feel how a tree must sprouting a new bud, not yet certain if it will be a branch or a flower, but absolutely sure that it is a new way of growing and understanding the world and that it has intrinsic in it an evolving sense of exploration.

The tree needs to learn and become conscious of both the air around it and that to which it is connected as part of its birthright. It is not even certain that this process will ever end, it may, it may in fact become old, or it may grow sick and withering die, but that is improbable, for it is a new shoot and it is fresh and full of the light and life of new beginnings. It may only die if it does not want to live any more, it may only die if it allows others to kill it.

It living and dying rest in its' own hands, requiring exactly the same effort. It is just a question of will. So that, one is not certain yet of the outcome, nor it's predicament entirely, except to say that it is inherently different to the others and carries within it a certain uniqueness, of which all are aware. This is something which it may find alienating and a source of great strength, even triumph. One does not know exactly, how such things can be known, but they are.

What I wanted to say to you, is that your effect on me, is to liberate me towards myself and enable my writing. You might think then that I am using you, but it is not that, it is just that very naturally and without any effort at all, this occurred. It has to do with all that beautiful poetry you send to me, when you communicate with me. At other times, through reflecting on you and how your words make me feel.

Sometimes, following these exchanges, something deep within me sets fire and alights. It is then, in that moment of absolute truth and longing for you, I am sent into the seat of my soul. Yes, I am marched into the depths of my being, where at other times I have fallen in despair, I now find myself rejoicing at our interactions, enjoying us, our union, our connection and level of connectedness. These all bring me here once more, to my writing, yet it is a different place to when I left it.

I can feel it now too, it is deeply situated within where I am and at last I have this great and overwhelming awareness of it all. I know now, where it is that I am supposed to be. How it ought to feel, being at one with the world and yet, at once separate. I know now, what it is to be at the centre of my being, as I knew even then, when I was here, yet surrounded in darkness.

Which reminds me, when I was younger I spoke about this at length in my blog. How it was such a struggle to come out of the epicentre of my being, because I understood that I could be surrounded by darkness and be there, or by light. That for me to forgo the darkness would mean such a great struggle.

At that time, I was depressed, self-harming, and bulimic. I drank copious amounts of alcohol and did anything to hide deep within the centre of my own destruction. Yet, while there surrounded by my dark, I still knew that I could feel as centred at the opposite end of the spectrum. I knew that the feeling was the same whether fully engaged or disengaged with life, perhaps that is why people fight to cling to their illnesses?

In order for that change to occur, I would have to struggle. At both ends of the spectrum the result is being at the epicentre of your being. The difference lies in what surrounds you, environment really matters. One understands such things very clearly in the middle of their own madness, such as they do also in the midst of their own sanity.

It was this awareness which caused my choosing between activities and laziness, between struggles and malaise, between head and heart and I chose heart. Thank goodness as my heart can now choose you and it has and does, over and over again, you, you, you.

So I went to a party and somehow that led to us being slightly estranged. It was a strange moving away from one another. This happened in spite of my wanting you to be with me. It came about in spite of my missing you, loving you and wanting you to be with me.

It is a very beautiful connection which we have certainly. I have never been so moved to such great closeness with somebody and I would literally die for you. I have never ever said that to anyone before and somehow it feels that everyone I was with before wanted that from me, except I couldn't give it to them. They tried various methods in order to string me up and failed, but you're different.

You're the one who doesn't feel that powerful desire to find me and make me yours. You are very happy with us bumbling along and facing our individual challenges until the time is right. I feel partly that this is so that we can get to be ourselves entirely before we actually connect as these two individual selves.

I am scared that we will never meet and my heart will break without you. I am scared that when we meet you will be able to love me and that I will cry and it will feel better than I have ever felt and that you really are everything I think, feel and know that you are. The relief will be immense and I shall sigh with such relief!

The difference between what went before and what is happening now, is that I am willing to risk everything for you. I have kept on having to do that and I know that I shall have to continue to do so and that is okay too. I keep having to stretch myself and be real and discover parts of me which need fixing, or to be loved. I keep having to let go of things and I am quite naturally letting go of people, ways of being and thinking and it is so beautiful living in your love. It transforms me and I am growing at last!

I worry that when I go out at night to parties, I will miss you more than you will miss me. I know that I already love you madly, for your words have saturated my being. So, the thing is that I often stop caring about how long it takes before we actually meet. Others whom I have told about you, are aghast at how long I have been waiting to meet you in person, but I do not mind. They judge me, worry for me and project all of their own ideas of right and wrong onto my own scenario.

I know this. I know that they may even be laughing and although I was once the very first person to care about such things more than anyone else, I no longer care a hoot. It is my life and I am living it in exactly the way that I want to and need and must and I would actually die for you.

I find myself already living for you. I do not care if that is an unhealthy way to approach life. If you ask me, it is a blessing beyond just living for yourself, when you also get to find that other person for whom you are living. This is certainty. All of the challenges which we are facing together already do nothing but deepen my resolve and understanding of myself and of you also.

I last wrote about you from my old home and have realised through having to move house, leaving my favourite tabby cat behind, that sometimes, life brings you close to others so that you can love them and that sometimes this is a short blessing, which has to end. I mean either way, we both have to die, which is a type of separation and yet also unity at the same time if you ask me.

The thing is though, that I see being human as a blessing because when you meet the woman of your dreams, by chance, you get to love them through that situation and then create space for that loving to continue and that is all within your control, while both of you are living.

The unfortunate truth is that as regards animals and inanimate objects also, we do not necessarily have as much freedom, because situations can dominate and tear us apart. The blessing of having met you is that I get to choose every single day to recognise what a blessing that was and to rise to the challenge of that, through reasserting and re-establishing my love for you.

Our togetherness is a part of my life now in such a way that whenever I look backwards, it is impossible for me to separate life from knowing you. I understand the desperation and pain when two people who love so deeply are separated.

I will never let that happen to us insofar as I am able. Partly, because I am so honoured by our love and partly, because I have no choice. Every single part of me, all of me, has been awakened by your light.

It is love which motivates me. It is your love which pulls me still farther and farther into the light and I know that for as long as I am being myself and you are being yourself, we shall be together. Which essentially means it can last until death and we don't even have to do anything differently, or behave in ways which are demanding of us. We don't have to change who we are, or how we are behaving, all that we have to do is to be ourselves!

In the face of such a beautiful ideal and way of being and sharing, I feel strongly that the views of my friends and people around me pale in comparison to that reality. I mean call me crazy, but getting annoyed at having to wait for you is hardly a priority given those sets of conditions and that reality which is already being shared and built upon. It is a far greater, deeper and more beautiful reality that I am waiting for, rather than rushing into the simple pleasures of sex and sensual fulfilment.

I loved it tonight when you said that you would love me always, for I am worthy of that love. That was one of the strongest and most beautifully written sentences I have ever heard. I feel so cherished when you are loving me and I feel that way all of the time now. It is the most liberating way of being that I have ever encountered. It feels like I have fallen into one of those black and white movies from Hollywood! Your writings to me are your song and we end up dancing together after all.

I have been fulfilled before in terms of sensual fulfilment. It was nothing on this. This is a complete full kind of loving. I am wondering whether you wanted intentionally for us to get through the whole infatuation stage before meeting, so that we could actually explore one another as we actually are, rather than just in terms of our ideas pertaining to how we should be? I am not sure.

I know that the universe loves me and protects me and that there are energies and angels guiding me and my actions. I used to hate taking time for myself, but now I no longer feel angry with myself for staying in bed whenever I do, or doing things in unusual ways. I no longer berate myself, or take responsibility for things outside of my control, because they are just that, beyond my control.

I am lost in you completely and love your spirit fiercely. You enable me being myself, facilitate who I am, complain about things you don't like and yet also allow me to challenge you also. We are exceptionally well matched my dear and I believe and feel and know and trust that our relationship, our union and subsequent marriage shall be built on the premise of mutual love, understanding and control, of ourselves for the betterment of us as individuals. This will of course lead to our greater freedom also.

This is what I suppose that old adage to mean, with great power comes great responsibility. If we are to be free, then we must take responsibility for our actions in the sense that they will always definitely affect those around us.

For me, how I deal with this is through great self control and this is also your way as I can see. Many of our ways are shared. I suppose that us being together is exactly what I have been waiting for and also in so many ways, it is exactly what I have been preparing myself for and working towards.

I always knew that being with your soul mate is the greatest gift and treasure and blessing and that only the greatest and strongest and bravest among us can benefit from such a divine gift. I find myself wondering whenever you send me another poem whether you really and truly feel these things about me. I find myself looking at your photos, again and again and growing increasingly excited about our first meeting. I am nervous too, because nobody really knows what's going to happen until you actually meet. You're the longest person I've dated without meeting in person and I am feeling quite old school to be honest.

Another thing that our loving has challenged and changed is my understanding of true love. There was a lesbian couple whom I knew. One girl was gay and the other was bi-sexual. They appeared to be very happy together as young loves dream and everyone was shocked when they broke up. The bi girl decided she wanted to conceive naturally with a man.

When she met her male love I doubted it all was real, although I hardly knew her and I found it quite distressing when she was celebrating this love on Facebook. I didn't understand that she may actually have fallen in love; I thought it all quite pretentious. I moved away from that crowd immediately, because I didn't get what was going on!

Anyway, in the end what happened is that I ended up meeting you and I realised that actually there are no rights or wrongs in love. All you have to do really is literally love as well as you can and we are all always inherently flawed and are naturally going to be making mistakes and that is okay too.

In many ways, it is like you are walking in the dark, with the most amazing person in the entire world. You both have flashlights and if you choose to hold hands or not, there are going to be times when you will meet with issues such as dirt which you trip over. Perhaps, one of you drops their torch for a while and you both have to stop to look for it.

Then there will be times when one of us will fall over. Sometimes fall flat on our face and get up laughing and at other times we will cry in pain and perhaps just not feel like getting up. At such times, the other person might try to get the other person to get up, or sit with them, or cry and so the other will get up to help them, to wipe away their tears.

There may be occasions when somehow we become estranged from each other, perhaps both wearied by walking together for such long periods in the dark, but we will not grow angry, nor fearful, nor lose hope we shall only grow hungry and thirsty and having eaten and drunk our juices and water, we may wander again.

Then perhaps we stumble and crying out the other realises that what they are really missing is the others touch. It might be the touch of the other's voice on their soul and how much of a blessing that that is. It could just be that all of the pain of the world disappears right about then.

Of course, we cannot always be talking to one another. It is just that in those moments, as we are walking through the dark, there can come times when we have forgotten why we are walking. Yet, it is right about then, that we get given reasons to reconnect.

Perchance, these things are happening. It is not that we are trying to engage or disengage either, but we do love each other so much that these things bring us closer and closer together. So that we end up never ever being too far away from each other.

Which is just as well really, because before you was death and I would die without you. I love you and I need you. Thank you so much for bringing me to life at last. I have been waiting for you since before time began. I think that part of the reason I am here as a woman and not as a man as first intended is because of you. I feel that much of who I am is because of you. There isn't even one part of me that feels that there's anything wrong, or incorrect in that statement. I would never have been able to hold, look at and eventually let go of my darkness if it wasn't for you. This is true and right and good as it is.

Before we parted ways, you brought light to my darkness when you were mean and unable to celebrate good things that happened to me in my life. I found myself desiring you to an extent which almost drove me crazy, which is funny because you did promise me this. Yet the parts of me which you targeted were my mind and body. You could not reach my soul because of your own struggles and fears.

It was the lack of ability to celebrate good things due to your own insecurities. I don't hold that against you. Your ability to deal with the darkness is what got me to see my mum that time I was so so scared of walking in to see her drunk again. Your heart is pure; it is your mind which is tormented.

You tried to get me hooked on you and it did work for a while. It may have worked for longer if you had left your house to come meet me. At the time, I was quite devastated, but then later, I realised we can only be who we are and do what we can. Here's what you did to my mind 'poshtulip', as you sometimes called yourself.

I shall always love you, for this is all I have ever wanted and been waiting for and looking for and hoping for and you are the absolute answer to every single question I have ever had and the answer to all of my dreams and without you there is no such thing as living and all of the other disparate parts of my life don't matter at all. It is only just you. I do all of these things of course and I shall continue to do so, it is not that I shall stop, or that I don't love being an actress and that being a writer is not an expression of my soul, it is not that at all.

It is rather that all of these things exist, but your presence in my life and your love and your being alive and present and here, all of these things are contributing to my ability to partake in these activities. It is because you love me so well and I suddenly feel like I am worthy of these things which I love doing.

I suddenly understand what it is that I am good at and love to do and I have this sudden urge and understanding that I am capable of doing more and of being better and this make me very happy, which of course also contributes to the capabilities which are manifesting.

The only thing is that sometimes when you are breaking down I can feel how distant you are. You have told me that you are bi-polar and I do not care. Sometimes you speak about self harming and I get so very sad, that I do try my best to help you back up.

You have called me on a few occasions when you were suicidal and I have tried my best. I have such great support from you, when I am speaking about my pain, hurt and bad times. Yet still, I am grateful for being able to help you with yours although yours is so much greater than mine and at times when you are distant I do worry for your soul and heart and all.

More than this though, I am worried about the good things which I have been trying to share with you, which you have been unable to respond to well. I have noticed that these pain you and so I find myself hiding these. I am not sure that this is a good thing to be doing.

Just the other day you slammed me for asking for help when your needs were so much greater than mine and it just made me think. It made me think about being trapped, alone in that darkness with you and if it wasn't for your writing, I might believe that this was all you had of yourself to give. You remind me of my mother, my Cancerian Instagram girlfriend.

AFTER

She takes a breath and suddenly all is gone. She has left her again. Alone. The world becomes a controlled place and everything makes sense. Except from how intensely her heart is screaming and the ways in which she is trying not to die. There is also a lack of something, some quality, some kind of light, of life and she has been left alone. She does not cry. There is no breaking. She is intent on making her point. Of lasting beyond this. Of going on. Somehow.

The bricks keep on falling and crushing her spirit and there are holes in her being everywhere, all over and she has to place her hand over her mouth, to keep from screaming each and every time she finds another space where she used to be. She cannot scream. For there is no one to hear her.

Everybody leaves. Nobody cares enough to hang on and ask her why, why does she feel like this. Even when, she tells people of her pain, they just look at her and tell her that it can't be real, because you see, she has never actually met her, so it doesn't count. It can't count when you love over the internet. What a farce.

Yet she's standing there. In her room. With her hands, both hands, over her mouth. She is screaming silently in ways that they don't even care to hear. Like always. Just like always. All of her life is escaping through those holes and there they are, slapping her on the back, asking of her to rejoice in the ending of something not yet real.

They do not ask her questions. They do not come close enough to ask, or even to see that she has not yet closed her eyes and they are red raw and glistening. They do not ask her questions, because they do not care for her answers. So that she does not care for them either, or their souls ways, or their unseeing eyes, or their uncaring behaviour. She does not care for them. Not anymore.

I had a dream a few nights ago which was so beautiful. I have been meditating to my angels as I always do and I have been asking them for very clear guidance. I am aware that sometimes our interactions burn us both and sometimes I get scared that it is the wrong kind of burning and I question my actions and I question myself and I question. They always answer me in the form of images and I know that you do not believe in such things, but I do. It appears to me, that however you believe in the Spirit, it manifests according to your will. This leads me also to ask you, are you happier without me now?

So, I had a dream. You and I were there and we must have known each other very well indeed, for I was following you easily and I do not follow. There was also a gentle grace and light about us, surrounding our movements, so that we appeared to me, both the dreamer and the one with you, as a good couple, with love.

We were with my two good friends Vicky and her guy, you walking in front of me on my right hand side smiling and I was following your hand in mine. It was a sweet kind of playful trick, with our fingertips chasing, you were leading of course. You turned to me gently casting me a sweet smile and we were walking down some steps.

Then, we stopped because Vicky and Joe had met an old friend. He looked like Gerard Butler, you looked at him and began walking down the steps towards him. I followed you, without the slightest hint of jealousy and then, when we had passed by, I could feel the sadness building in my heart because you were attracted to this man.

All of that sense of worthlessness began to arise at the realisation that I could not compete with a man, much less a beautiful one, just then you turned to me. What you told me put my mind at ease, because you had only fucked him. You said this and with your eyes told me that you had been in a horrible state of mind. You certainly did not enjoy it and as only dreamers can, I knew this before you spoke.

I hope that you do not feel badly of what I am about to say, that you hid the truth. Instead you said to me, you recognised their friend because he used to go to the places where you went to when you were into the darkness. I looked at him and saw the mask he was wearing.

The pretence shone in his gait and his laughter suddenly seemed like he was ripping from somewhere deep inside. It all made me feel sad for him and I kissed you and told you how I felt. How grateful for you and how selfish it is, but I was so scared, so very scared that you had some feelings for him. Although I did not wish that truth, I was still grateful for it and wildly so.

In my dream, I knew I could not tell you that I was aware of the whole truth. In my waking life this happens to me often also, where I have intuitions which I cannot share. Lately, I have stopped fighting against them and instead have begun feeling blessed by their guidance.

I listen not only to them, but also at how I resolve these hints at life. When I am free to share them with those around me, these gifts proliferate and my friends and

I can rejoice together. At other times, not being able to share may be a warning in and of itself. Therefore, I have learnt to listen to everything that happens in life. It is all meant to be heard, understood and acted upon somehow.

In that moment, all I was able to do was to make you feel safe with me. To make you feel like I believed what you were trying to tell me and that that was okay. I wonder now where I was in any of our relationship. That dream highlights for me how so many features of how it went wrong and could not have been right.

MINE

Of course, I was grateful after we broke up, because I discovered that you had been stealing your writings. The same words which you used to steal my heart. I know now that we were never together; I was betrayed by a fallacy and lured into your dream.

Yet, I learned so much through sharing my darkness with you and I finally felt accepted because of it. So that you gifted me my own self acceptance as well as the realisation that the darkness is not the important part at all. We are.

I want you to know that you can change the world for the better, that you are capable of that. Your movements, your own personal dance of freedom, joy, pain, suffering, love and lust and being as you are, in all that you are, can and does help people to live. The world is full of both light and darkness and the only way forward is to bring whatever is in the dark to light.

You have been doing that, since before I've known you. It is in this way that you helped to heal me too, though at times the lessons were excruciatingly hard, there were also the most beautiful miracles of thought. I love the gifts you sent me, even the words that were not yours, were still meant for me.

I have a great understanding of your heart and soul and truly wish nothing but for these to win their fight against your corrupted mind. I want for you to be allowed, enabled and fully supported in your healing process. You have suffered enough. The important thing is to let go of the labels which you were given by others, all those words within which your darkness is captured and allow yourself to heal without them.

I wish that your mind was not sick with bi-polar and your heart not shredded from abuse and that the drugs they gave you didn't make you high and then low, so that you sleep every evening at 8pm, often crying yourself to sleep. I wish that somebody somehow could have protected you from your past.

I wish you weren't anorexic, that you didn't become an addict and you never knew you could self harm. I felt all of the pain in your stories like they were my own and I told you things which I thought I would always be afraid of telling someone.

You liberated me from so many fears and removed all that stopped me from being intimate. I was looking for someone like you, who I could share all my darkness with and there you were filled with such beauty and light. Except that then I found out that I couldn't share my light with you.

So that, in the end it was not your past that broke us up, it was how you behaved in the present. It is because you were too nervous to come to see me. It is because you did not want to, or wanted to too much. It is because you were too unreal. I would not have cared if you had told me that you had selected those writings for me, because that is equally as sweet. However, because you did not, it became apparent that you were wearing a mask, so that I actually loved someone who partly remained hidden. Or parts of different people and that is okay, but it is certainly not you.

On your birthday, I give thanks to the universe that I got to meet, love and share, with such an exceptional being as yourself. That I was walking by your side and now am here and grateful to the universe for your strength and light. You are the one who encouraged me to face my fears on my mother's birthday and to go to see her in spite of every inch of me saying no.

You made me realise that even if she was drunk and wasted, this is not something to fear. You made me realise that my love for her was stronger than my fear, which was predicated on our past. You sent me a voice note for her, which I greatly appreciate. I am not sure that the look on her face was in order to please me, or she was being genuine, but it was a beautiful moment.

I have found so many great things in the time you gave me and I am eternally grateful to you that you always had time to help me out. You always listened and I love that we both enjoy sharing to the same extent.

Among the shame in what occurred between us was though is that, when you actually did write to me, I overlooked it. This must have hurt you so badly because it did take me a week to respond to it. In retrospect you see, it did not have the same rhythm to the writings which I was used to. I did not realise why either, until the truth came out much later.

I felt betrayed because these things which you sent me were part of why I was so open with you and felt so deeply for you. It also hurt because I knew, that if you had just told me from the very start that these were not your own, none of the fallout would have happened. If so, then maybe we could have had a chance, but what's written is written, et cetera...

I thought at one point that you were the most beautiful creature alive and I would have died for you. I thought that that was what love was and that I would die without you. Now I can see that love does not demand anything, especially not that you lose yourself, especially not that you suffer.

It gifts you everything which you could ever desire and I know that in many ways, is this what you were trying to do. The difference is that these things did not come from you, which is as beautiful as it is destructive, for both of us.

Yet still, should you read this, then please listen to me when I say, take off the mask. Stand naked and tall and in all your ugliness allow your beauty to emerge, like a child does from under the blanket house of its dreams. All of our creations deserve respect, in adulthood and in our youth, but we must not allow ourselves to become subservient to them. For they are not alive, we are.

She came for a moment as a coating of dew does in the morning in a world that has not yet woken up and as it is awakening she is there glistening until suddenly she's gone.
Sometimes though, the beauty in natural occurrences are that they find their own rhythm and it's up to you whether you wish to be present or not.

Top left: Age 12.
Middle: Modelling age 16.
Bottom: With my extended foster family age 16. Opposite me is Greg my foster father. I was taken into foster care only two days before my 16th birthday which came as a great shock to me. The social worker came and took me away. I remember my brother running after us when I was driven away, screaming my name.

Thankfully these Earth angels (my foster parents) contributed to my healing, although it still took years. Greg was the first father figure I'd known and was a kind, strong gentleman.

Top: Age 16 at the peak of my struggles with Bulimia. You can see how thin my arms are & how my face is swollen from being sick. **Bottom Left:** Age 18. **Right:** Age 20.

11 BETWEEN TWO WORLDS

The Constitution
It was the beginning of the day
The rhythm was not yet formed
But it palpitated, knowing
Its own existence

I am the one who has risen from the darkness of oppression, of the self and have stood standing between where I was, where I am and where I had hoped to be and smiled. I am that. I am the one who ran frantically from this experience, to that, who screeched, screamed and scratched every single pathway clear, again and again, until all I really wanted, was to be forgotten. I am that.

I am the one who fell to the ground so many times, that it appeared to want me there, to be the only thing that truly wanted me. I am that thing that believed that nothing was possible and so, I would be lost forever. I am that. I am that one who argued with you for hours, because it distracted me from the pain of still being alive and even then, fought against you so hard that my pain, inverted, became our reality together and we could no longer be. I am that.

The first world is the real. It is the one which we are always sharing, it does not change, does not alter. Whether we be walking through it with our eyes wide open, or shut and whether we believe in it or not. This is the first world. In it exists weather and days, along with concepts such as children and adults. Here you plan your weeks and keep your diary free, you budget, or don't and they take your home from you, or award you for work well done.

This is the world of features, of featuring us and where our acting, our ways, our wardrobe and how we hold hands can become front page news. This is the world of air-planes, fighter jets, jobs and worth and value built on time, ethical standards, money and love. This is the first world, where you can see what you've built and know who you are, in relation to, in relationship with, as another.

The second world is the invisible world, the world where you learn how to build what you feel. Where you come to understand who you are because of that feeling in your heart and those feelings deep in your gut. How you relate to one another, how you love, how deeply you love. This is the second world, the world of knowing. Knowing who you are, where you're going and why.

Knowing how to be, who to become and who it is that you wish to share that journey with. It is this world of which you are part. It is that state of being which only you can know, it is this entirely subjective reality which you can introduce other people to, but which only you can know truly. It whispers to you, deeply into your soul and into your way of being, feeling and understanding. It is your resonance within yourself. It is your very own unique truth, patterns of behaviour and understanding. It is your forever self. It is you.

Your inner dialogue, your loves, your passions, your feelings, your souls emanations, your uncertainties, your definiteness, your insecurities, all that you embrace, all the worlds which are interacting within you and all the ways in which you are interacting within yourself.

We see only what you are given to sharing of the second world and sometimes, the world can seem an arid, barren place, because we are missing you in it. Perhaps, you have gone to the second world and gotten lost, or we have forgotten that you are so much more than the first world and we have lost you in confusion.

Sometimes, our minds thoughts betray us and we cannot find you any more, even that you are here, standing right beside us. We are saddened by our perception of your having left, when really, you have just lost yourself and so have lost us also, or perhaps we have lost ourselves and so you also.

So, now that you know that there are two worlds, let me tell you where I am, how it is that I came to be between them. I think, personally, that we are all vehicles for energy, the workings of spirit moves within each and every one of us. My mother beat me to channel the stress and pain of the suffering that she had endured, because she had been so hopeful that she might get to love someone, somehow and not being able to pain her so much. She loved me so much that she was scared and was so scared, so terrified, that she broke in all of the ways that we all hope not to.

Of course, that was her cage, her trial and tribulation, it was her yet it was not her. This is the same woman who loved and nurtured me, with such great strength and power, such gentility up until I was five, and I was always happy to be by her side. It is the first woman who I ever loved, my mother, aside from myself and yet, my love of myself was silent, my love of her spoke through all those days of suffering with her through all of her torment.

It hurt, it cut, it bit at me in such a deep and hard way that I bled all over the place. It was not me bleeding, it was my experiential self. It was my dreaming and nightmares about why we were such worlds apart that I cried so often. When all you want to do is to love someone, it can create a huge insurmountable chasm; it can break you from the inside. We both in our ways of wanting to love one another, broke and did not manage to allow ourselves to do just that, so great was our need.

Now, I can see two things from this time, firstly, I am grateful for that passage into her pain, sorrow and suffering. I had a free ticket through her pain and misery, as only a daughter can and it was not mine, just as it was not hers, yet still, we got to share it and she took me from my heavenly viewpoint deep into the darkest trenches of realities lived and journeyed through. Yes, yet still I am here as she is and we are starting to thrive, at least relative to where we once were. We have not changed, but the journey has.

My point is that had she not have beaten me, then how was I to go there with her? I see this all as a mechanism, a key into places where we cannot go without permission, which is granted to us by those around us. There are many worlds into which we can try to enter, but others hold the keys. It is always up to them who gets in.

This is the point; I am between both worlds, because I no longer belong to either. The first world has many, many things which I love, certificates, grades, books, but books which often lead into the second world, where many of my loves are also. Like ideal, like infinity, like trust bound up in oneself, like deeply resonating sounds and feelings and ways of being... like magic. Yes magic exists. There is a depth to each world and in many ways they mirror each other, in many ways their paths diverge.

By being in-between I have the good fortune of being capable of seeing both and benefiting from their lessons. The issue with belonging to neither is this sense of knowing both far more and far less, than those who belong completely to either. It is a sad; a deplorable state of affairs, yet still it is filled with liberation and joy. For, I am always aware that I know so little and also that I am always willing to share all that I have. As my actual setting in life, in living, is one of absolute insecurity, I have little to lose and less to cling to. I am alone.

I have queried this sense of aloneness. I have wondered if I am not imposing a reality upon myself which is not actually in full existence, but of course this is not so. Saying that I am alone does not mean that other people do not exist; I am merely accepting that all exists in relation to me and where I am, both inwardly and outwardly.

That it is through this being, that I get to experience both worlds in all their forms and that my journey is just that. It not absolute, it is entirely subjective and implied and restricted through who, what and how I am and all that I cannot know. I do not mind, how can I? When I get to live between both worlds.

12 DYING UNTIL DEATH

It loudly cries in my mind
the sound of your moving
from deep within.

Death came very quickly upon her. It came in the moments when she didn't really want to address life. When she hid, silently, easily, gently, under the rock of herself. It was addressed far more eagerly though, when thinking that she might die soon.

Today she had felt that, had felt the carpet of life being swept from under her feet, or perhaps tugged might be a more appropriate adjective, for she fell gently and quietly. It was a sort of tumbling downwards, an encircling of self, yet still she survived. She had hardly realised it what was going on and had hardly felt it happening at all. It all came about so suddenly. Then again, that's what happens with death I guess.

You would think that the idea of death and dying would drive people away. However, what it does is that eliminates those whom you don't want to be closer, from your path. It removes all this pretence that we are going to live forever, making you more real. This is what it does for you.

Death is a gift then. I am not saying that the suffering which some must go through to get there is, not at all. Neither am I saying that it is glorious, for most it is an absence at best, at worst, full of the torment of losing, or having lost. Rather I am saying, that all life gives you tools and using these we might find our way towards betterment of self, with a much deeper understanding of how things are, among these our own selves.

Thinking like this has brought upon a flashback. One of a beautiful blonde with pretty curls, which danced around her face while she moved. One of a person for whom life is dancing with her and she is on the verge, always, of sitting down, or getting up as a result. It had happened shortly after their meeting again that she had slipped. Her legs had buckled and she had creased, eyes closing gently.

The whole world had melted away from her then, luckily we had caught her. Luckily we had all been there to catch her. When she awoke I was holding onto her hand. In that moment, I am certain that she understood everything, but as the saying goes, you cannot take a horse to water.

There is a stillness now, inherent in the world. Now that I have thought about death and it has been addressed and accepted. It might not happen quite so gently you see. It might be a sudden immersion into the light, or a quiet wrestling with the unknown. I am doubtful though, most likely, it shall just be a gently sliding proceeding.

I am not aware of anything except that it builds up slowly, like how ivy creeps and grows up piping next to your home. Or perhaps how ashes slowly accumulate along the mantelpiece above your fireplace, supposing you do not have a person who's cleaning it quite often. This may be how death comes gathering to you?

I think maybe, that death is our friend. I think that

she positions all of us into a certain context and surrounds us only with people with whom we are grateful to know. Placing us with beings who truly matter to us, with sounds which resonate and others for whom, no matter what, by their side is where we belong. I am nearly certain to die soon.

Of course I do not know, my mother was the same, forever assuming that death was closer than it was. For you see, this is far easier in many ways than expecting ourselves to live forever. We do not know when it is coming for us, even as we do not know where it is that we are going. Yet still we can be safe in the fact that those whom we love, love us equally too. That we are in love on equal terms, that we do love like that. In this sense then we are guaranteed to die in love, which is a most pleasant way to go, knowing such things.

Also, as a Scorpio, we like to think and speak about death quite often. It is something which grasps us firmly; it is all around us and reflected in the faces of those, both younger and older, who are walking among us. One cannot but be faced with death quite often. If we are at the very least honest with ourselves, then it is something that we most of us ought to be considering far more than we are. The fear of death and what's going to happen to us afterwards would be a far better way of maintaining safety and preventing people from abusing their power of being human, I feel.

I am quite naïve, but then quite often it is the gentle reminders which are built on truth, which have the most power, in my experience. I have tried many other ways, but this one worked best. The other thing that works really well is instilling a sense of gratitude for life in people.

Now, this of course, does not and cannot result from a life filled with fear, doubts, anxieties, suffering and pain, much like those on the periphery of capitalist experience. Also, many who are doing quite well have these feeling as well, so it is not exactly like the system enables one to feel secure.

Therefore, one needs an emphasis on better ways of living and being in the world, no matter what your place is on the social ladder. It is not that you may ever lose your place as yourself you see and once this truth is instilled among humanity, it is something that ensures a certain level of security, calmness, peace and even joy, regardless of external circumstances.

The other thing of course is, that you are aware that the most important thing about being here is sharing our experiences, which are modulated by who we are. Therefore, once we have ascertained that it is who we are, that has value, aside from what we may or may not have. Then we are immediately free from the imposition of fear, shame, anguish and many other possibly maladaptive surges of feelings. It is better, that we all live in peace, side by side with each other and our own selves, with all their death and glory, then that we strive to live forever, with our inner selves dying daily. Don't you agree?

That day with the girl with the blonde curly hair was a moment of truth and real intimacy. I have noticed that there are many others like her now surrounding me. Real people, who truly and honestly want to engage with you on human terms.

It is important to allow life to grow inside of you and between shared spaces which you occupy. If you are engaging in activities with people who don't facilitate your joy, then they are adding to your sorrow. It may be better to let them go, so you can live. The question is if we choose to live while dead inside, isn't this the real Death?

13 THE ONLY FAULT

Decisions
Liberty is ours
We say such things in jest,
Hands interwoven
Like grains of sand on the beach

The truth is that I love you. I don't know what you were feeling when you got undressed for me. You made me feel shy and inadequate then, but I know that that was due to a slight immaturity on my part.

I know also now that you were probably afraid, as fear makes us more sexually aggressive. I know all of these things now. It was premature for me, sleeping with you then, I wasn't ready and that's because I wasn't just looking for an experience. I know that.

I know now, that I truly did like you, but had you not have gotten undressed then I certainly wouldn't have gone there. What of it you may say? Well, all of those feelings which you were trying to get rid of. All the ones you were trying to shed even as you did your beautiful clothing remain. There's nothing either you or I can do about that I'm afraid.

You have left me now. I realise this, how it feels, how it actually is. Perhaps you're mad at me, because you nearly died and all I could do was text and answer your calls?

It may be that you missed me in all of those hours. It may be that you thought of surrendering yourself to me then, yet I was still so far away. Then I came back, but you have now left this space. It is not empty at all, it never shall be, for it is our space and it will remain eternally occupied by us.

It may be that you want to get remarried, that you have chosen this man in my absence. I understand that also. It's not like we are the only ones for each other. Not at all. I believe that we all have many possibilities.

Yet still, I feel that you don't realise that for me, it is not about all or nothing, it is about having everything you want. Getting all that you need and if that means having multiple partners then so be it. It is not necessary to reduce the amount because that is what the world dictates we ought to do!

The truth is that capitalism has stripped us of so many natural decisions, so that we follow it into the depths of all that it is and make only those choices which it requires of us. Yes, this is so and it is as true as our love my dear. You know how I know our love is true? It has not petered out. It does not matter that I did not see you for eight months, or more even? It does not even matter that there was somebody else, because I knew. I knew it for all of that time, even when life rushed in, with so much love for me, I could not deny the truth, of us.

There have been others too, it's not like I have been sat here waiting for you to come to me. Certainly not! I have been out and about, loving as always, yet still it does not and apparently can not diminish our love. That is the truth at this moment, now.

Yet it's a truth I do not know what to do anything with. It's a truth which I cannot do anything with, because it is as part of me, as you have become. With your wonderful ways and deep open heart and beautiful shining soul full of such love and delicate honesty. It was hard for me, to come to you last time. On the premise of our new friendship, as if words could wipe the past clean and reclaim the land of our true love for fodder. As if anything new ever comes about through words, except perhaps newer suppressions and in our case better expressions.

It seemed that the deeper within we hide our love, the further back we pushed it, the more intense it became. I am uncertain whether it has become more intense now, or if it is just more real. Yet now it your turn to disappear. That is your choice as well. This time last year it was you who were so certain and I who was running.

So I'll let you go, even as you had to let me go, leaving it to life and the universe to settle our allowances and repay our debts to one another and the others. For there were always others between us. You know that. We both do and it's part of the reason our times together are so desperately sweet and intense.

I wonder what you're doing now? I'm sitting here at home listening to *Ciara's OH*. There was a time when I was reticent to invite you to my home; I was quite ashamed of my lack of affluence. I wonder what it is that made me have such a great big chip on my shoulder, but regardless it has gone now.

I am enveloped in pure joy at being able to continue on this wonderfully strange and uniquely beautifully exploration called life. I have truly never ever been as happy, as fulfilled and filled with love and light as I now am.

That means that whatever I have, I am happy to share which includes my home. It also includes my heart as well of course. I am very lucky to have many wonderful and beautiful people around me at the moment. I just want to be able to love them as well as I can, because they are all magnificently wonderful. Honestly.

It would be great if we could catch a coffee soon, but in many ways I also don't care, for that's no longer the point. I am free. You are free. We are all free and it is just this that enables our sharing, from a truly good place. Not because you are wanting to possess me, own or have me, but because you are choosing to spend your time with someone whom you love.

That is the truth. Why should I try, as I have tried so often in the past, to knuckle my way into your life? When you are a fully grown and very beautiful and intelligent woman, who if you want me, shall let me know!

Why would I want to try to be somewhere where I'm uninvited? It makes no sense to me any longer, although in the past I was so desperate for certain individuals to love and accept me. Now I can see that I just need to love and accept myself and I do, which is why whatever you do is superfluous.

It is not just about me either; I also love and accept you in entirety. This is why whatever you say to me I am fully accepting of and always will be. That is where I am at now you see? So you do not need to give me any of your time and attention. You may marry this man, or another, or you may choose to never ever speak with me again, I do not care about such trivialities.

I hate for you to think that I am mourning for you, when you have chosen to be with another. I hope that you truly are straight as you tell me. I don't know. It feels like you are trapped due to your culture and wanting to please your family, but I don't feel comfortable assuming that you are a lesbian closeted by circumstance. In many ways it is simply easier to believe what you have said. Instead, I choose to just observe without accepting or rejecting, for I may never know.

It is not as if I am bereft, for the very act of loving is not limited to any particular person. It finds its expression elsewhere, in how well you love other people. It explodes out of my heart at times in hugging others, in making art, in song, in dance, in happily laughing and sharing stories with friends.

It is not that I am using my loving you. It is beyond all loving in that it needs not that you do anything at all really. As yourself, in existence somewhere in this wonderful universe, you have already unlocked my loving and there is no longer a key, a door, or a place in which to put it so that it is but spreading itself merrily all the way through me and out into a world which it breathes love for and into.

You as an individual have given this love birth, as each person we love sets new parts of our loving and ability to love free. It occurs through engaging with something and also somehow everything that they do, say and are. It is beyond even the they that we see in the mirror, or walking, whom we hear talking and laughing with all those beautiful locks bouncing and falling delicately around their face. Hair which frames your divine features, illuminating your high cheekbones and fantastic bone structure as they do.

Indeed, you are wonderful, but what is best about you remains to be seen, heard or understood in our primitive tongues, or ways of deciphering truth and gleaning meaning from such depth. It is not that you are beyond comprehension, let us not go so far, but that your spark remains untouched by its being comprehended or not. It simply is. Even as you are. Even as I am. We all of us having our own individual light. All of us having our own particular ways and beauty. It just so happens that yours touches mine and shines from within me with absolute certainty of its loving.

I have never been merrier than now. In reverence of your being. In adoration of that spark, yet I know and get that you're absolutely human and we are equals, we are mere mortals indeed! Yet still, this feeling does not change, nor my heart stop shining and radiating goodness.

I truly think, that out of all my ex's your heart has

been the bravest yet, which is why it is shocking to see how eagerly you follow your mind and fear. Sometimes I think that the mind is an awful device, though mine has become my friend, through adversity.

Don't misinterpret what I say though, please. I understand you are a Leo and used to take some of what I said as far more complimentary that it actually was! I found and find this trait endearing, nearly all of my ex's have been in love with themselves. There is nothing more beautiful than waking up next to a woman who loves herself completely. To be honest our waking up together was slightly awkward, but that's another story!

It is not that I am living for you as some poor ignorant and misled person does for their "other". Be that a person, a spirit, a god, or money. Certainly not! I am here for me and me alone, I am even here to serve and help others for me. I am loving because I choose to be, from a place of absolute understanding, where loving is heavenly and not to, hellish! So you see, my character and her choices are my own. It is but that you have graced me in the same sense as Dorian Gray graced those two men in that novel. Something of his soul touched their's, but it was they who saw it. It was they who understood beyond what they could see, the absolute goodness of him and of his character. The version before the painting I mean, although some might say that afterwards he became more real, I prefer not to draw any comparisons between his murderous self and your light!

Although you might not mind at all, loving yourself means you also get to laugh at yourself. Thank you for teaching me that. As younger women we do learn much from older ones and you have taught me much about self love and self exploration. I remember when you asked me whether I had ever slept with my hand cupping my pussy and how red I went!

So then, what have I come to say to you, who is not and never shall be mine. I have come to tell you that I

120

am absolutely and entirely loving you for always. Nothing more and nothing less. Of course, it would be nice to see you, nicer to hold and kiss you, for I do recall that your kisses are heavenly!

However, should that not occur, there's nothing lost. We have had everything together already through ever even having shared our space and I shall remain eternally joyful in many ways as a result of our loving, of loving and of life in general.

So it is a fabulous way to be, loving you freely, even as you have the choice to love me. You said to me that you love your dog very, very, dearly and that you need not have her to know it. How true that is, yet still how much more blessed your life is when you get to hold her in your lap. When you do get to stroke her and show her how you feel through your touch.

How more fulfilling a relationship is, when you have both time and space to share those silences, scaring intruders away with those funny faces one makes. When you do not want to be disturbed by an outsider, because you are so in love with loving in that moment, with the person with whom you are sharing that loving. How certain you are, that others who are lesser in the sense of the depth and resonance of your connection, won't be able to hold and fulfil that very same sanctity of yours.

How resolute and determined that you shall retain it for as long as possible! As determined as children are when they have a new friend and their parents come to that friend's house to take them home! How easily children share that they are neither ready nor impressed with their parent's intrusion. How readily such things are shown and discussed, how much animals too reflect this inclination and at times also those who are in love.

It is like this in life, if you do not show how you are feeling, then those feelings don't get their true time in life's meanderings. In a sense, they are not only not given life, they are essentially also driven to find their place for rotting somewhere inside of you.

This is horrendous, given that whatever you have in life, shall be taken from you when you die anyway, so why bother holding it inside where it can be your poison? What of death too? Do we not die a little each time we do not give? Is this not the actual pain and suffering of life?

I went to India and the children there living on the streets do not suffer as we do. They do not try not to give of themselves as we do either. There's definitely much pain, it is not that they wouldn't prefer another kind of life, but there's not that same wretched desperation which you see on the faces of so many here. Bereft of themselves, because they are fearful of loving. I was scared too and I have told you that.

Now though, I am also loving quite freely and it is a liberating time for me. To be able to give of myself now, more than ever. It is not that I am incentivising your loving me, you understand? It's just that if you are afraid, it is not worth it darling. It may seem egotistical. That is neither my intention nor how I am entering into these thoughts. It is just that I am grappling with your behaviour and actions, trying to elucidate the reality which they betray. I may be failing miserably, but at least you are getting to know me better.

Yet now I am tired, for it's three-thirty in the morning and you are probably having mad passionate sex with your lover boy. Indeed. I am not at all jealous. I have had much mad passionate love myself and was jealous when it was not truly love, but a form of possession and deepest lust and infatuation. I realised later that I was made to feel insecure through manipulation or truth, for we were not well suited, now I know better.

It is funny how quickly we learn what matters to us, when we are pushed into lives which we do not want, with a person we tried to make ourselves fit with through our minds. Strange too how much you can love without it being pure, yet how purely you can love and know it shall never, can never and will never end. I am just learning.

Regardless, I am writing this merely to say that I hope you are happy. I am pretty certain that you are, you have such an amazingly pure heart I cannot believe otherwise. I would also like for you to know that although you were part of the reason I broke off my relationship, you were not the only reason and that I feel no inclination to demand anything of you, nor do I have any expectations. I am just happily living my life in as open hearted a fashion as ever.

Of course, I do love you and I shall probably always love you. I cannot help myself nor how I feel. I cannot shed those feelings, they are always growing with and within me, as only love truly can. Naturally though as time passes and takes up the space of days lain in between us, so too shall the feelings become platonic. I enjoy such changes, I welcome them and with these also, new friendships.

I trust that this message finds you well. Filled with love and truth and the awareness of your own beauty and how very loved you are by many. I shall no doubt be quite bashful if we meet again and discuss this letter. Yet I do not care about these things now. I am far too aware of death to fear loving and too loving to fear embarrassment, or any form of discomfort where such beauty is concerned. For I love you and what could be more beautiful than that? I wish you only the best in life, loving and living. I wish you all the wonderful things.

Should you wish for me, in whatever capacity, I shall simply be honest, without debilitating or in any way harming myself. I have told you already that I am inherently selfish. I am also shy, contrary to your belief. I cannot tell you how many times I came to meet you in the student bar and got distracted into speaking with all of those people about whom I care little. I did it rather than have you looking into my eyes and realising how much I love you. It is such a hard thing for me, trusting people with that intensity of feeling. At least it has been up until now.

Now though, something integral has changed. I have spoken to enough people and been loved well enough to open up myself completely to people who might cause me harm. I trust life fully. By harm I don't mean maliciously, but you know how love can hurt?

Well it's nonsense! Not loving hurts!!! Bad maladaptive relationships hurt!! Love doesn't hurt! So the harm I mean of course is a leftover miscommunication from my youth. When my mother caused me more harm than care to divulge and left me with this sense of what "love" was. Of course, she never was loving me at all when she was causing me harm. I know that now. I can see all of these things now, as clear as day, but it has taken time.

During that time healing happened through the BSc degree in Psychology and my true passion for acting, yet most was through loving women. I have to be honest. Women are the most amazing creatures alive! Even the ones I would never go near again, have bestowed me with such fabulous gifts. They have taught me how to love myself. I am the woman I am today because of the love of women throughout my life.

Yes, it began with my mother's tender loving care and then it was down to the many other women to love me. Which they have, I am uncertain that there is another person alive as loved, blessed and lucky as I am! Certainly towards this latter part of my life that love was more sexual and deeper emotionally, but you see it all matters!

Yes. Women have healed me, taught me how to love and heal myself and how to be a good strong happy woman! It is so fabulous honey! Really! I shall go into more detail with time. For now, goodnight and I trust that this message shall find you well and that you will gain much love, light and beauty in reading it. As too shall those who read my book with an edited version of this inside, obviously without your name, Goodnight for now.

14 NEED

Accolades
If it was the emptiness
That caught me out
It was also what
helped form the greatest
Impression in you

I needed you then. That was the problem. You couldn't have anybody needing you, did not want that at all. I think perhaps if I had my time again, I would try to hold back a little. Would that have helped? I'm not really sure, maybe, maybe not. Who knows? When you enter into the darkness with only a torch, sometimes you stumble into a brick wall.

I have learnt from my past and that is why I am behaving as I am now. Towards you and everyone. It incubated for a while, the feeling, until it got a chance to see the light. Now that it is here, it is magnificent in all its splendour. This is its time to surrender to the light of awareness. I am not afraid of it any more. It is just a feeling and as such, it has yet to be explored properly. To do that, I feel it important that I take you back to where it all began.

I am a young girl. Somewhere between six years old and eight or thereabouts. I have always been a good girl. Once I stole twenty pence from your purse to buy sweets. You caught me afterwards and I lied because I was scared of your reaction. I remember that it must have been the summer holidays because there were lots of children s laughter coming through the door.

It must have been quite a punishment for me then, what it was that you chose to do. You may have hit me first, I do not remember all of your slaps. Certainly you grabbed me and pulled me upstairs. You did not have to do either. I would have followed you, had you have asked. It appeared that my feat was beyond asking and answering questions though.

Once upstairs the punishment was given. I was to use a hard bristled brush, to scrub the wooden landing of the stairs which was black with dirt, until clean. You probably showed me how to do it. I probably cried for days. The worst part as I remember it, was not knowing how long I might be there for. So that the moments carried themselves into aeons of time.

I have always been a good girl made to feel bad, inadequate and wrong. That is okay though, now that I can see the untruth in these suppositions. Now that I know how fully wronged I actually was, it is all okay. The only thing that is not okay is this feeling that I am left with. Yet, I have found the place from whence it came. I can see it. I feel it. I know where and how it was birthed and therefore, can fully accept its trajectory in my life. I need only travel backwards just a little in order to find it.

It is snowing outside again. It is nearing the end of March in 2013 and it snows. Delicately, like it's reintroducing itself to an old friend and lover for whom the door never closes. Sometimes I marvel at how very beautiful life can be. The girls are in the kitchen speaking in Polish and I delight in that fact. I will not go there and it is all because of this need inside of me and where it began. Let us return to its space fully now. I am ready to show you how it all started. I am ready for you to see all of my insides. Please, come with me.

I am a little girl, with afro hair and a cute little smile. Later in my life they tell me that I was very beautiful, but I was always too busy feeling and thinking to realise. Usually, in Ireland, when you called at people's houses they would say that you were "gorgeous". I didn't buy into this for a few reasons, the first being my not feeling as I thought somebody who was gorgeous ought to.

The second was that they appeared to call everybody of a certain age that, so its meaning became so diluted in my mind; I felt it but a fancy nicety. The third was the most prominent, such words always came before an offering of biscuits and like most children do, I loved biscuits! Some things come to overshadow words meanings in a child's mind. Like the delightful taste of custard creams with some Barry's tea! But I digress.

I am a child, who is very in need of love and wanting affection. I wake up and it is Saturday morning, which means two things. It means, no school and it also means that I may get to sleep next to mummy this morning! I smile in my bed, turning over and listening carefully.

Now, the thing is that mummy doesn't like it when I get into bed with her. I know this already. There are times when she yells and shouts at me for moving in the bed. Times when she demands that I get out immediately, as I have been moving around too much and disturbing her sleep.

At such times she likes to sit up a little and hiss at me. I cry when she makes me leave. I just so want to be near her. To lay by her side. I really want to be held, but as this never happens, I simply yearn. Sometimes, I manage to sneak into the bed and she is so fast asleep that she doesn't even notice! I delight in these moments thoroughly, I am made very happy. I lay there grinning broadly, filled with all of this love and joy. Whenever she moves though I must be absolutely still and quiet. Should she realise I was there, or ought I give her any reason to explode, she will.

So I am very aware of how close to her I am laying. I get up as close to her as I possibly can without upsetting her. Sometimes I try to breathe her in, she always wears the same perfume; Estee Lauder's White Linen, it a smell that I have grown up with. I identify this smell with love and safety and as an adult have a tendency to always buy the same perfume. She is wearing hers and its scent has mingled with that of cigarettes and alcohol. I breathe in the heavy scent of her, as I have always done. I truly love to be as close to my mummy as possible.

I love her very dearly and am aware that the only way to truly love her is not to allow her to know. For the moment that she becomes aware she growls, under her breath, barking at me to leave. Immediately, I become a whimpering thing, filled with such need. It took years before I fully understood that it is natural to want to be loved and to share love. That it is normal to want to be closer to those who you love.

Quite recently it struck me that I have an issue now in that I have this need. This need is unfulfilled, will always be, because it has only to do with her. I am so cautious now of getting too close to my mum. So absolutely maimed by this early experience of love, that I must revisit it now with you. We must go there and see exactly what has happened, so that that wound may heal and I may move on.

I am in my bed now, having just turned around towards my door. I stretch, last night's dreaming still quite prominent in my mind. It was a good session. I have this sense of absolute gratitude, peace and love. I do not know where they came from, as I fell asleep wailing into my pillow again. Begging god to give me to another family, that they might be able to help take care of me.

That I might be able to come home every evening after school and do my homework like all of my friends did. That I would not have to sit for hours inside or outside that damn smoke filled pub with Radiohead's' creep blasting out every time I have the courage to pay the jukebox to play it. I sit in tears, nearly in tears, or I run away to the toilet to let them spill forth.

Sometimes mothers friends come, telling me how much she loves me and why am I crying. I feel so bitter inside and frustrated at their incompetence at pretending it was their choice to come speak with me. I feel so angry, that they have bothered to come outside and find me in the rain, where it is cold, but at least I can feel that and know that I exist and am not inhaling putrid smoke.

I feel so angry because they have chosen to be here beside me, under false pretences and I want to puke all over them, I am so disgusted. I would sit there and decide whether or not to go along with their bullshit, meanwhile my feelings were curdling inside of me. I was curdling inside of me and the taste was bitter.

I still haven't mastered the art of consistently going home at night and I am quite a bit older now. Yet, as I am so enamoured with learning and have been all of my life, I am always studying in one way or another. Which is good, as it gives me such clarity and direction.

It is not that I would be lost without it, but if every day were the same as the last, I may lose my ability to appreciate difference. I have learnt that through times in my life when I have had to work harder for money. It is not the work that is debilitating, but that sense of sameness. In truth though, even this has lost its power over me now. I know enough to see the differences, not to have myself be overwhelmed by either apparent changes or consistency. It is not at all what it seems. The passage of time and our envelopment in life is what moves us.

I am laying there thinking. I jump up, readying

myself, it is cold. I breathe in and the cold air cuts a little at my throat. I am wondering if this is going to work. My door is easier to open than hers. They are both heavy, but hers has a sort of latch whereas mine has a door handle. I twist mine, lifting it easily and gently. She doesn't make a sound. I tiptoe into the landing, which is absolutely tiny. It is literally just the space between those two doors. I wait there for the courage to take me further. It is a long waiting, although only short in time.

The snow is falling heavily now, blanketing London. It makes it appear so pretty and clean at last. I love the snow, but this morning I woke up with this sense of foreboding in my heart. I understood that there was a darkness, which I had to deal with. It is such a difficult thing living as me sometimes, because the wounds of the past come to you for healing at the most inopportune times.

You become aware that you must be evolving as a person, growing healthier because emotions are triggered and with these, memories. Then, you must just take the bull by the horns, allowing and enabling yourself to heal. You must look at those wounds in whatever way is most gentle and they will be well. Trust that and be brave.

I could've tried dealing with it last night, but I was so damned tired. I am hardly eating again, coupled with the gym, my essay and this writing, I suddenly became exhausted. The snow is plentiful, like a store of love. My love is endless, it also melts away and takes on other forms. At the moment though, it too is like the snow. Covering the world, my world, making everything apparently beautiful. It also comes from nothing into nothing. It also comes at will.

I have decided that now is the time. With all of my might I stand before her door. I have wrapped enough fingers around it to be able to move it gently. My breathing has greatly reduced. I am holding my breath. I pull and it makes a sharp sound, before squeaking open. I pause.

Silence.

Rejoicing I open the door, ready to inch my way in over the step and into my mother's bed. The door's still moving backwards when I realise. Her eyes are open. They are wide open, staring at me. The look that they hold is so dark, I feel endangered. My face flushes, cheeks burning, as I can feel myself beginning to shake. Her lip curls. I am such a bad girl. I am such an ugly person, that even my mother hates me. I didn't expect for her to be awake and now I have nowhere to go.

"What, what is it? What do you want?"

The want is spat at me with such venom that I jump. I can see a slight look of satisfaction in her eyes. Her face is holding onto my fear well. She understands her power and loves to abuse it. A tear trickles down my left cheek. I reach out my hand towards her. I am so choked up, that I cannot speak. There is no room for words between us. There's no space for me to say that I love her. Please, why can't she just love me too?

"Well! What is it? What do you want you stupid little girl? Hmmm? You want to come and sleep with mummy?"

Mummy also travels with its venom laden high. It sarcasm hits me across the face; I am hardly breathing and want only to die. There is a lump in my throat which is threatening to choke me, I pray it hurries up. My hand drops.

My head hangs low, yet I am still looking at her. I cannot take my eyes off hers; they are so very angry and burning with so much hatred. Where did it all go wrong? What did I do? You used to love me, I remember. You used to hold me, to hug me; you used to speak with me so gently. What happened! What did I do?

She half sits up in the bed. I do not know if I want to runaway, or run to her. Neither is a viable option. I am half dead; she has killed my heart for loving. My legs do not know what to do. My mind is heavy as my heart and I am weakened greatly. I do not understand. I do not understand. I do not understand, yet I know that I am afraid. Why did I come here? Why did the door make such a great big noise? I hate it! I hate the door! And I hate myself! Stupid, stupid girl!

This moment when she is choosing whether or not I am allowed to enter is the hardest. There's a part of me that wants nothing but to go there to be with her. There's another part who understands that being there is not enough. It is never enough; there will be more pain, but no satisfaction.

There will be awkward silences as I lay there trying not to move. If the duvet cover goes off me, I will not ask her for it back. I will not even try to get it back. I shall try not to shiver and make any noise to annoy her. I shall try not to. It is a hard time. If I fall asleep too, I may be woken by a kick because I have moved far too close to her. Perhaps I made a noise, or touched her. She doesn't like to be touched.

Now when I sleep with my partners, I cannot understand her absolute aversion to being touched. For me, it is one of the most beautifully intimate aspects of being alive. Sharing that inner space with somebody, that sanctuary. I am as grateful for their trust and understanding as I have ever been. It is not that my early experiences with my mother's vicarious ways have tainted that aspect of my loving. For once I am in relationship, then all is well.

It is still that moment where you are standing outside their door. When you have left your space and comfort and are stretching up, trying to open their latch. It is still the suspense as you go to open their door. Is it going to creak too loudly and wake up their inner demon? Are they going to be angry too? Will they hate you? Will they decide that they no longer want you to lay beside them? It is not the act of their deciding which is hard, for when you are there in that moment you just act.

The panicking comes from not knowing how they shall respond to your love and loving. This is the thing. This is the reason that we are here together. To see what has come before, to let it be as it was, so that it no longer tries to be more. To become more and more visible and overshadow the present predicaments I am in.

For, the choices which I am making now are getting purer and purer, as I am getting closer and closer to love and to that same person who I was before. It is not that I have changed exactly. It is that the things that were done to me had never really been looked at by me. Now that they are it is apparent that these wounds exist and need only to be tended to with my own awareness. After this, it does not matter so much that they have occurred, except in the sense that I have lived through them and moved past them.

Beyond my own healing, I know for certain that until my mother sorts her life out, I can have nothing of hers. I have realised that I have to vet and filter, all which she tries to give me in love. This may be part of the healing. I do not think that anyone who is healing wants to be in direct contact with their aggressor, be that a human being, a dog, alcohol, or their own dark thoughts. It is not that we avoid them altogether, but that we are facing them on so many levels already that their physical presence is entirely unnecessary.

I am healing. That is my choice. I have been healing for years perhaps, but now that love has sprung between me and another, I must heal. So that the burdens I carry, do not cause harm. I feel like isolating myself, so that I can inspire and enlighten, rather than harming or cause fear or confusion. I want only to love freely and well! That is why we are here.

My living well necessitates my absolute freedom, as also does my loving. So that now, it becomes apparent, that this is actually the true need of which we have been speaking all along. It is not the need of a partner, nor affection, it isn't the need for money, clothes or food. It is not even the need for travelling, learning and having fun. The need is one which all of the people I know are hungering for.

It is the truly good vice, belonging to those people whom never stop growing. It is that of loving. That is the need. To love. To be loved is absolutely wonderful, yes, but loving freely and being loved freely, as our own true selves is the true need of which we have actually spoken.

I thought for many years up until now, in a way that I wasn't consciously thinking about it, but rather mulling it over, that it was love which I needed. Now I see the fallacy of that way of thinking and how mistaken I was to feel like that. It was so ignorant of me not to understand that it wasn't that I wanted her to come into my heart!

Not at all! I wanted to go into hers, because I wanted to be able to love her. I always want to be able to love people. I can see that now as we are here speaking. That was why I would mull over entire conversations in my head as a child of eight, nine and ten years old. Finding myself unable to sleep at night due to my awareness of what I had said, the effect it had had and how that might in turn lead to different responses.

My youth was full of the antagonistic responsibility of a being too aware of their choices, the possible outcomes of what they said and did and the isolation that burden of responsibility invariable brought. That is why I would want to play only with specific people, joining in their games and fun.

I am always selective with the people who I want to love, understanding perhaps something of the fact that our time is limited here. Also, although everyone can accept your love, few are actually changed by it. These are the ones whom I spend the most time with.

Sometimes, I couldn't though. I understand now why, because it hurt me then. It hurt to spend time with people who I truly loved, because I did not understand much of their language any more. I had not been allowed to love for such a long time, that I had gotten lost. It was becoming far easier to be around the people that didn't love fully, than those who did. That was the truth and it was painful.

I still get that wave of feeling sometimes now, often it lasts for a day and I must escape those whom I am with through writing in order to hold my own hand, allowing myself to manage and know it is alright, everything is alright.

I suppose, I must have this inclination towards isolation as a protective feature of my being. In all honesty, when I find a being with whom I can be alone and not feel that they encroach upon my isolation, then I shall be with my soul mate.

I must confess I have a very strong feeling that they are already around me and it is such a liberating experience knowing I get to love them and that they get to love me without pretence, games, fears, or any form of pressure. It is the most beautiful thing that has ever happened to me and I have never been so grateful for someone else's existence in my entire life.

Which is not to say anything beyond it being a miracle and every time I think of her my eyes well up with tears of gratitude and my heart beams love. I never thought I was worthy of love, nor that I would ever be able to love again. Due to my extreme sensitivities and strange nature, given the proclivities of my upbringing and mixture between wealth and poverty, inside and out, it seemed so impossible.

Now, I give thanks daily for it all, for she gives meaning to the struggle, which is ongoing, yet diminishing the more I get to know her, gladly. There is a saying by Kahlil Gibrain about how when we weep in sorrow we must realise that we are weeping for that which was once our joy and this is exactly how I am feeling, but in reverse.

The snow is coming in wisps and I am about to

make some tea. I wish to tell you two more stories which highlight the effects of not yet having looked at what had happened. One involves a trip, the other a cigarette break. The latter isn't mine, it's been ages since I have smoked and although from time to time the whiffs I get in passing are nice, I do not miss their effects. The trip may or may not happen. It really depends on quite a few separate events. It is not whether or not I go that matters though, as much as how I reacted the other day to the idea of going.

This is the point, that to remove yourself from reality and dwell only in ideas, is not a good way to live. I have been living in such a way for years. It builds a kind of force of pain, which only awareness, love and acceptance can melt. Then, just like the snow, they form rivulets in your being and can truly begin to nourish you! All of our experiences are such, should we only choose to let them be.

So, what is it that I have to share with you now? Last night, quite a funny incident occurred that has subsequently made me more aware of my behavioural tendencies. The girl I was working with, Barbara and I were chatting. She looked at her watch, I immediately said that I was going to get a drink of tea. She called me up on it asking me why. I was like, well, you obviously want to go for a cigarette, so I'm just going to have some tea beforehand.

It all got quite funny then, she became rather annoyed. She was like; did I ask you if I could go for a cigarette? I'm like no, but you obviously wanted to go! You were looking at your watch! She's like; whenever I look at my watch you get so upset. I was like, no I don't! She's like, every time I look at it, you do that, you disappear! I said yeah, well what's the point in my bothering to stay here when you're looking to get your nicotine fix? She said to me, why are you getting so upset? I was like, I'm not upset, I just pre-empted your action. Silence.

I came back and stood beside her, but I really couldn't remember what we were saying. She said that that's what had always happened. That every time she looked at her watch I would disappear. To be honest, I hadn't really thought about it before until then, but she was right. It suddenly struck me how strange that was, to pre-empt her actions. As if so scared of being dismissed, I would dismiss myself first.

I am beginning to notice a similar thread of behaviour in nearly all of my relationships apart from with partners. How strange and wonderful. I pre-empt their rejection of me, by leaving first. The thing is that now that I have seen it I realise how untoward it is. I mean, yes, she was thinking about smoking, but did she really want to end the conversation then? She actually said to me;

"Yes of course, I want to have a cigarette, but I can wait for two minutes, it's not a drug!"

Of course I corrected her on her last point! Funny the way we think about the things we love, which we have need for. When she was going for her cigarette finally, she said something rather touching. She goes, don't be upset with me, I don't mean it like that. That sentence really touched me.

I realised how important it was to go back to that place that made me feel like she was rejecting and dismissing me. In actual fact though, if that incident wasn't building on two previous to it then we may not be here at all.

The most important is the one I referred to earlier, is that of the trip. Basically, I went home for a day to celebrate St. Patricks day. While I was there a friend of a friend invited me out to her birthday. It was a very sweet invitation actually and on that same night a good friend of my friends was having her leaving party and the girls were celebrating something.

I wanted to be there, as I wanted to be closer to this friend. It was important to me to understand whatever it was that was growing between us. What did it mean? Anyway, it wasn't so much a thought as my heart wanted to be with her. So I said that I was going.

When I got back to London, I tried to book but the server kept crashing. I was messaging her all the time, back and forth like that. She wasn't responding, so I waited. Then it got to the next day and I sent her a sweet message.

It basically said that I needed to save my money, so couldn't afford to go. I felt relief when I sent it, waiting for her reply was so hardcore. Then she responded saying that she hadn't replied the night before, as she was at work until late. My heart sank when I realised that it wasn't that she didn't want for me to come.

I had taken as the ultimate rejection when it wasn't at all. It was simply that she couldn't reply at that time. I know that she loves me, why then does spending time so close to her make me afraid? So it was this thought which was floating around in my mind yesterday when this thing happened.

Also, my friend who I had taken time looking after and I met on the stairs. I had so much news that I was bubbling over with it. Then she stopped me, saying that she was really sorry and could we meet for coffee later in the week.

I got such a shock, which really hurt me. It wasn't anything to do with my having taken time to look after her; it was simply that she didn't have time for me. That still hurts now; I have no interest in seeing her at all actually. I have pushed her away.

Later on that same day she came downstairs to give me hugs. I pushed her away and asked what she was doing? She said that she was so grateful to me for looking after her, that she wanted to hug me for a while. I said okay, because I understood that she had realised what she had done. However, at the same time, it's like; you should be there for me when I want you, not just when you do, right?

Well, anyway, that's how I feel. That might even be the reasoning why I didn't like her when we first met. Perhaps my heart and soul understood that she had this great capacity to hurt me. It might be that, or it might be that she had this great capacity to love me also! Life outlines its reasoning gradually over time and we get to experience our real truths over time and as we grow older.

Now, the last instance of which I wanted to speak also happened at work. With the girl I spoke of earlier, we were standing outside by the reception. We were speaking about this girl I saw on my visit. Then I said that I didn't want to speak about it anymore. Nearly immediately afterwards I left her side and came and sat in the back by the cloakroom! She came in after me, smilingly and saying really? She gave me quite the surprise with her strong jovial voice.

My attention captured, she proceeded to speak; you came all the way in here because you didn't want to tell me? Really! You didn't have to do that! I wasn't going to ask you anymore! So, you see we both burst out laughing at that. It was simply delicious the realisation of one's own extreme reactions. Of course, it is all about trust really. Yet, without that reaction how was I to realise I didn't trust her?

Also, how was I to fully understand why I behaved like this towards certain individuals, if it wasn't for my being made aware of them by these people and circumstances? You know what too? It's not always a comfortable experience, being made aware like that.

Sometimes it hurts; sometimes it's unsettling, sometimes it can tear you apart, a little, or a lot. You know what else though? It's like the physical realm, certain types of surgery are invasive, some are keyhole, others are for the sake of settling your mind and making you truly feel more beautiful. They all have their reasons, their causes, their uses and they are all necessary in some deep way.

Somehow, afterwards, if it is really healing which is taking place, then you feel stronger than you ever have before. That is what it is all about really; growth, learning, loving, accepting, healing and allowing life to take you by the hand.

Thank you for coming with me here. I really needed to see myself as I was then, to see her, to see and know us, so that I could walk away. It is only when we are fully able to let go, that we are capable of fully accepting all that we have been holding on to. Then we truly are free to grow into the beautiful beings we really are!

The snow is truly magical. I was so gruff with it this morning; it hurt me to see it because I was in such pain. Then came the light and so gradually I was able to appreciate its beauty. Then came the seagulls and I was finally able to soar with them too...

I am free, to enjoy the experience, as any and all, without Need.

15 DON'T YOU

Ancient Times
It's foggy outside
I can't see a thing
But I can feel
Alright?

I sat my first exam today. It was quite a tough one. Not necessarily due to the material that they test you on, or even those questions, but more so about the way in which the pressure affects you. It is now Wednesday and last Saturday night I cracked. I simply could not handle the sheer volume of unknown predicaments I was surrounded by. Every single pressure that you can imagine was there around me and I simply had nowhere to go.

The funny thing is though, that in actuality, the pressure had already been alleviated a little. The day before my brother had transferred some cash into my account. I believe that they were right when they read my fortune and said that my single greatest difficulty in life is accepting love. I am certain of it. It sends me into a sheer panic at times.

I guess it must be left over from the idea that you

can lose your love, that a person can stop loving you. I don't ever think that anyone can go through quite as much trauma as that feeling brings. That constant awareness. I spent years fighting to get that back and I failed. I don't really know what that says. It is a strange thing talking about it now with you. I can feel the pain in my heart where it's tender. I could cry, that's how my body is reacting, but the thing is that this is far deeper than any tears ever go. I am wondering about the idea of each year blanketing us, just like each of the layers in an onion. How many blankets deep are you, dear feeling?

I sit by the window in my bedroom. Directly in front of my window is a tree with the greenest leaves ever. A man stands not so distant from my window, speaking in a language which I cannot discern and there is such beautiful piano music in the background. I do not yet know myself and I never will. This is understanding and acceptance. I spent so much time bound that I had forgotten completely what it is to be free.

When I was walking home today, with no panties on and I could feel my bum cheeks sweating in my bright orange tights, I knew that I am alive. The man across the road, with the most fantastically bright red and white flowers, looked like he'd never lived a day of his life. His face was ashen gray and deeply and they were lines of burden rather than happiness. I felt suddenly pained at the idea of his going to a funeral and turning the corner, looked away. The truth is, he may as well have been going on a date, the procession is the same.

It is one of those beautiful evenings, when your thoughts simply desert you and you are left only feeling. It might be the lack of sleeping over so many consecutive evenings. It may be that release of stress hormones, dopamine, serotonin and sweet oxytocin as I sip on my coffee this delicate evening.

I had promised myself not to fart in my room in case she arrives, but of course I just have. It's okay though, it's really not that smelly. Something similar happened this morning too before she came. We embraced and it was still coming out of my butt cheeks, but she was so happy to be hugged that she saw beyond my dimpled grin.

For my part, I enjoyed that delicious unknown cheeky moment, but I did not think that I had 'gotten something by her', as I might once have. It was a different sort of sensation, that of pure enjoyment at life. The innocence of enjoying our moments is so very refreshing when we are able!

I took a sip of some of our seed water before going to the shops. The other part of "we" no longer is living here, in this city. She is very far away according to maps, but I know she's just right near me. I sipped that same water we had shared before her flight and I walked some of our journey from that day. I think maybe I was dancing inside when I realized how well I had kept her with me, within me, I can see her face so clearly now. I didn't realize that we were on the tips of being in love at all; it has only just recently come to light.

The thing is, of course, that even being in love, doesn't mean at all that you are meant to be together. It is just that you both have that capacity. I am not the marrying sort, but of course if she wanted to get married I would. I would happily marry her.

Not now though, but then, you know, at that time when it all makes sense. Right now would be impossible! It is, quite impossible, but she is on the verge of where I can see too. Her red hair is sometimes blonde or dark but her eyes are always bright, she smiles so prettily and has that same laugh.

There is something about a woman's laughter. I catch their laughs and make them my own. Quite recently though, I got quite caught out and now I am considering making mine silent. I was happy with the random wheeze I had acquired through crossing over quite a few different sorts.

I was happy until I used it today and the invigilator, who had been into me up until that point, abruptly, looked away. I suddenly became aware of the absolute value of my laugh. It is a good thing that it was just with her and not one of the beautiful creatures I usually have around me.

It is not that we are all having sex you understand. In spite of our attraction to one another, I am quite shy. It is just this that has led to many women getting frustrated with my behaviour. I seem quite extrovert and outgoing, but of course I am really this vulnerable, shy, ruthlessly and painfully introverted girl. I mean I am also a strong, courageous, confident woman, but I am always breaking. I do not know the ways to follow to get things done, that come so very easily for everybody else. These ways are not my forte.

Also, I don't follow very well. This has its advantages and its disadvantages, a disadvantage being that you cannot gauge who I am, how I am, or what is happening where I am. An advantage is, that I am free and people love being around me as a consequence. I am also scary because of this though and attractive in a strangely curious way. Different people react towards me differently.

There is a tulip on the bedside table. I can feel love in my heart as I write of it. It reaches the arms of its stalks up towards the window, its' head tilting slightly upwards in anticipation. I am wondering if that is how its' soul left its body when it was plucked and now it's dead corpse has fixated in this pretty stance. I am wondering why they pluck such beauty, without realizing that they cannot capture its' essence. Is it not better to leave it out in the wild to wither with time?

Or would leaving it be like a person, left by its soul mate due to a fear of the responsibility that comes with looking after something that you have chosen? Is it that same story? If it is, then surely it is happier in here with us? But then why must it reach as it is? Has it been left reaching as it did when it was going home to the source? If that is it, then I envy it's reaching. I am still growing wild and the wilderness is becoming staid and boring somewhat.

I wish to be plucked, shared in closed yet safe luxury. Loved with absolute attention, care and kindness. Not the loving to which I have grown accustomed either. That born of words, with faulty habits and actions attached which run out, because they are built on falsities and pretence. No thank you very much!

Stay there, with the others who are lining up behind you! Why do you think that they must wait there? I am absolutely without fear. Why should I keep them so far away? It is not too far, I'll grant you, for they do trickle inwards gradually. Particularly, at the end of days, or in times when everything goes soft and they are aware.

I just moved the laptop. The thought came into my mind that the light has changed, the thing is though, is it the light that has changed, or I? It must be me, truly, for what light changed a person's attitude towards a particular place and way of sitting? Sometimes it just doesn't make sense staying where you are.

The phone goes intermittently with various texts and I respond. I am remembering now that this is also what she said, the psychic, that I was to respond. She intimated that when I tried to execute plans and "make things happen", it only came across resistance. She was right then and was also correct when she said that I ought to let my feminine principal guide me. She said, that when I enabled my male aspects to dominate then I wouldn't be able to harmonize. I didn't really understand what she meant, at the actual level.

Later on, when I went down on her, I was still thinking about that. She was furry, but her pussy was small and I remember that one of her hairs was adamant about staying in my teeth. Her husband wasn't at all impressed when he returned to the room. He wanted me to suck his cock, it's quite an awful state of affairs when a couple are competing for the outsider's attention, don't you think? Well anyway, I got bored after that and made my exit.

Every now and again they would reappear. Until they didn't any more. In the beginning, I felt bad for her, she seemed to really care about and love me, but then I realized that these things are nothing relative to hanging on to someone else's neck. He had made her into his puppy, she was not at all compliant, but he had full control. I see it now, then it looked so different, but I was naïve and luckily, too good.

The room is heating up now and there is condensation on the pint glass that holds the tulip. The girl who gifted it to me is a vegan. I sometimes wonder what that really means, except that her mind tells her to be good and she tries very hard to comply.

It seems that buying dead flowers, murdered flowers, is hardly the activity one would associate with a vegan. However, having said that, her bringing that flower into my room probably saved part of my soul. I was feeling a little sad and ungrateful about being alive, yet because of her gift she has inspired me.

As a result, I remain grateful to her now, I shall retain this feeling for her throughout my life I am sure! Such occasion's birth love inside of me every single time I look, both at them now and inwardly towards them later. I think this truly is a beautifully marvellous experience, this being alive, moreso to have been enabled by experiences to recognise this privilege.

I sat my first exam today. It wasn't what it seemed; I thought it was about attaining a result when really it was about living through the process of experiencing it. I think this is a common mistake to make, don't you?

Above: Still with Johanna as 'Tanya' taken from breakthrough crime drama indie feature film *Red Devil* (2019) Directed by John Pavlakos and distributed by Phoenix Worldwide Entertainment www.reddevilfim.com/ Watch the trailer: www.imdb/com/title/tt4898564/

Below: In *Disquiet* (2019) playing 'Sam' a Smartphone obsessed millennial, in this short film about the extremes of digital addiction www.imdb.com/title/tt10004258/

Top: Poster from *The Good Boy* (2018) with Johanna as overbearing mother and night nurse 'Maria'. **Middle:** Still from the short film *Psychotherapy* (2018) with Johanna as protagonist & psychopath 'Rachel'. **Bottom:** As sociopath 'Susana', in *Bricks of the Wall* (2019) at the Etcetera Theatre in Camden. 'Johanna excels as Susana, bringing complexity and allure to the role' – review by Everything Theatre.

Top left: *Fashion Meets Music* catwalk show in LA, 2017.
Top right: Johanna modelling at LA Fashion week 2017,
shown with designer Isabelle Deringo from Switzerland.

Middle left:
Green carpet
premiere for *The
Wind Cries* (2018)
with Australian
director Alistair
Marks. **Middle right:** Ecommerce shoot for Jose Hendo's
eco-friendly brand with clothes fashioned from bark.
Bottom: Film still from *The Wind Cries* (2018) which
premiered at an Oscar qualifying film festival in LA.

JOHANNA THEA

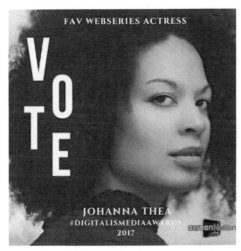

Top: Nominated for 'Fav Webseries Actress' for Screennation in 2017.

Photo by Jennie Scott Instagram @jenniescott photography

https://www.jenniescottphotography.co.uk/

Middle left: BTS still from a shoot for Nicole McMillian Hair.

Middle right: Final image from a shoot for Nicole McMillian Hair.

Bottom: BTS doubling on the blockbuster *Ready Player One* (2018) for Warner Brothers.

Top: BTS as the lead's venguful daughter, the Shaman 'Jasmine' on the Italian dark comedy/horror feature film *Fuck You Immortality* (2019) shot in Northan Italy.

Middle: BTS on short film *Struggle* (2018) as Mrs. Mole with actors Jonathan Hansler & Donna Combe.
Bottom: Beautifully naive, Johanna in a homemade costume, before a casting for *Game of Thrones*, before she learnt that costumes were not required for auditions.

Top left: In a world renowned members club in London, Johanna with one of her closest pals, fashionista and estate agent Leva Junkere.

Top right: In Lough Gur close to where I grew up in Lower Grange Co. Limerick, Ireland.

Right: My closest friends; Dani, Olga and I during one of our hangouts in South West London.

Top Left & Right: Johanna with her dearest friend since childhood, meghan, in Lough Gur, Co. Limerick.
Middle: Johanna with her grandmother Anna.
Bottom: Johanna with her Irish Step-grandfather Mairtin, grandmother Anna and her brother.

Above: Nude from 'Lets Talk About Sex' series by photographer Aleksandra Karpowicz **Below:** Cover girl for *Diva Magazine* 'The Sex Issue'.

16 THE GAME AWAKENS

Defensiveness
Pertains only
to the melancholia
of rejection in one's youthful
times.

They were all sitting around the kitchen table when it happened, when it first started to grow. It began with a growl and a rather innocuous one at that. It was shared by those around the table, as one does a shudder, or a yawn.

The latter being more appropriate, so let us stick with this miraculous thought. It was an unconscious and invisibly shared yawn. It may have been invisible but it was certainly felt and everybody felt it when it was beginning, especially the boy.

The boy was young, his eyes sparkling with an intelligence and curiosity of someone far senior. He looked about him always with an air of sprightly dignity and until that moment had carried the legacy of his entire family in his stride. But then it happened you see. It happened to the boy who was young and glistening with his intelligence and youth.

It captured his edge and started to melt it into something soft. It what which had until that very moment dazzled every single person who had visited that house, with its purity and innocence and absolute strength.

It took his edge. It took it away in many, many instances, but all of them, every single one, began with that moment and that moment is what we are referring to as "The Awakening of The Game". For, this is not the thing that has been taken, but what it was that existed exactly up until the second of that happening. Let us look into this a little more deeply.

It was a cold blustery day in that household, yet everything seemed fine. The baby was unusually placid and complicit. The mother was joyful and loving the chance she was getting to speak so freely about her life and feelings to her friend. She was like that anyway. Absolutely beautiful when life took a hold of her. Delightful when animated and always animated when delighted by listening ears. It didn't take much to fulfil her, does it take any of us much?

The truth is, that with all we have to feed our bodies; we have so much less to feed our souls. With all that we are given to believe we can take possession of and find pleasure in, we are actually enjoying so much less of life.

So would you really judge her simplicity in enjoying truly sharing her life? What other pleasure is there that is greater really? What other love is more pure and liberating? Except perhaps the love of dance, but let us not enter into that debate here, it is rather endless and pointless as we aren't yet capable of interacting at quite that heightened level beyond words.

It is time for us to return to this household now and rather than dilly dallying any longer over context, let us enter into it at last by saying that the father is out. He is working and has been so since early morning. The previous night the house had had a party and so it is rather interesting, that although she is so very happy, there is a deflated feeling to her voice.

Her movements betray the beers and at certain times she has taken to twitching slightly. It is not an unusual, or in any way awful twitch. It does exist though and it is remarkably pronounced in her mind. As if a large axe were wielded before her in each instance, making her defecate. Her facial expressions appear thus and at times I am given to laughing.

She joins in too, so that we find ourselves laughing together often. Yet like me, it hurts her to stay there for too long. Too many things have happened to her, for anything to be taken lightly. So we are letting go of it at least three minutes before we have run out of laughter. We are making it stop. Ending the fun.

This predicament makes her stand straighter, each time searching with greater and greater ferocity as if for something lost. It might be something which she feels should be cut, peeled or left elsewhere, for it is cooking time. It is cooking time, even as we are all cooking, meanwhile, the events of the previous evening are starting to spawn this thing.

It is the ending of our laughter, in absolute prematurity. It is the grace which is leaving us as dusk descends and the animals once enlivened, stalk into their respective corners, leaving us in that house alone once more with the darkness. There we are, all of us three, with this thing that we have created. This reality which is becoming increasingly more and more, pronounced, as the pressure to create an absolute culinary delight mounts.

Personally, I do not care for food. I have cared, then life told me to give up on it and I let it go. More recently, sharing cooking has become pleasurable once more, but you know that it takes time and attention and unless I am in love, it is not my thing. Then, at that time, I did not truly know love, so it was for me to not care. She cared too much and I did not care enough.

The thing was fed. I think that the worst thing that anyone can do with an unconscious stirring of one's mind is to leave it unattended. We did this unwittingly. Nobody had told us that we create more in our concerted efforts not to do, not to see, not to be, than in our actions. We thought that we were making food. All the while we were making this thing.

I nearly cried at one point. The laughter was so hard we were screeching, all the while starving the truth, satiating our lies and spewing it all into the immeasurable thing. The very thing which the boy would encounter and being the weakest link, regurgitate in its finest armament. He wasn't to know, we wished only for his safety. We tried so hard to protect him! It was ridiculous! We were bursting that's how hard we tried! But nothing could save us from our own creation.

The Awakening of The Game occurred at exactly seven thirty in the evening. At seven o'clock he had arrived home and was particularly hungry. We sobered up at the thought of eating all of that food. We were both privately angered at having to eat. One of us had been anorexic, the other bulimic, both with the intense desire to starve to death. We had self harmed. Cooking figured into our list of self harming, because we would either not eat it or puke afterwards.

Either way it was all a delicious form of torture. Akin to all of those beautifully colourful magazines, with all of those ladies whose upper thighs remained wrist size, no matter how long we stared. I had sought solace in many things, but really and truly, pain was the only true delight. We had all failed by having upper thighs which were not and no matter how hard we tried, refused to be, anywhere near wrist size. We were pissed.

For us, life wasn't about family and children. It wasn't about holidays, cars and promotions. None of that mattered shit, all that mattered were wrist sized thighs and concave stomachs. We were angered by only eating food.

We were supposed to starve, that was our legacy, our only promise to ourselves. It made us so perfect. We were perfected in the act. The act which we attributed to our betterment.

I can't tell you how many drugs I've taken to get to wrist sized thighs. Funnily enough, the closest I got to that was through unreservedly starving and exercising without alcohol, or illegal drugs. It was different though as I was super young then and had given up totally on life. Depression certainly makes it easier to destroy yourself. Anger, anguish and hopelessness don't make it a pleasant ride, but you take what little comfort you can in the idea of your dying soon. To that end you focus all your efforts.

Afterwards, bits and pieces of joy and fun kept popping up and into my life, so that I could never fully return to that level of the distress and self destruction. I have since embraced all the joys of living and have since risen beyond the scars. I have since grown. Yet back then, I ached to die. Death to me was not the ending, but the perfecting of myself; it was an image which teased me ceaselessly.

So you see, it wasn't as if we were cooking through our love. It was a feast borne of the anguish and anger of two of us kids and our restricted expressions of pain. Not because of anything, except that we couldn't realise how hurt we were, how would we continue living then? How would we go on, if not cloaked in that blanket of pretence and hurt?

We didn't know how else to be. There were no true models. None who could show us how to be. We lived in the darkness of a self-medicated environment where nothing was enjoyed except pain.

We lived in a world where only pain itself was safe, because we were certain of more of it. Therefore, we took it upon ourselves to create our own. We determined to feast on our own ribs, borne of that excruciating self perpetuating need to self destruct.

Eat yourself more and more and more. Just keep on eating away at yourself, so that no one else can. That was how we lived. In that day, our ignorance and pain, our fear and loathing birthed The Awakening of The Game in that boy.

The youngest of us wasn't the boy. It was the girl, but she was so much younger and bathed still in that effervescence of new birth, was protected. We were all loose cannons and he was cannon fodder. Oh how I regret our illnesses. How I regret them enough to script them that you might also learn of our wrong doing and inhibit, or choose beyond your own re-enactment of the same. Be strong people, for it may be coming for you too.

We were three then, the baby and that poor young boy. Three fully grown children and the young spirits sat there too in complete innocence. I feel that we were acting innocently, but because we chose not to heal ourselves, we weren't actually innocent. Now we are, more or less, but it's too late.

The Awakening of the Game has already happened and it is busy perpetuating itself elsewhere as we speak. Be aware carriers of The Awakening of the Game. Beware those who harbour malice and remain unaware of when it takes their children, younger siblings, aunties and sasu-ma's. Beware. All of you know better next time. Know better this time too.

So listen, we were there at the light brown stained kitchen table. The food was covering it and it was all manner of "Badness". All the foods eating disordered people cannot handle without freaking out were there. There were chips, of the skinny variety, mashed potatoes, ketchup, mayonnaise, there were fish fingers deep fried and other vegetables too. It was the most innocuous thing that did it. It is never the evil lurking that causes the most harm, but the good that facilitates its doing.

The plate crashed to the floor. The first omen, as her face grimaces. I grow afraid. There was that same horrid feeling in my stomach and yet I had no ability to stop any of what was about to happen. He takes his right hand and grabbing a fistful of French fries shoves them into his mouth. It opens and closes loudly as he's chewing.

I can see all of those millions of calories piling themselves in on top of each other. It is horrendous watching them breaking apart and jumping out, attack the rest of the food on the plate. Sometimes they lodge little pieces in their master attack upon the innocent, lower calorie vegetables. Although, you see, we no longer care, the point has come in the meal where there is no getting away from actually eating. We are all stuck at that table, glued to our seats, imprisoned.

We have turned all of those pieces of food over a million times on our plates. The baby has been cooed at so much that it's just sat there grinning. It would be a malicious grin if we didn't know any better. How can she choose tonight to foil our plans? We are looking at each other. There's a note of understanding before we tuck in.

His mouth is splattering it everywhere. Ravens are making noises outside the window, in flight. They seem to be cackling at our pain as our stomachs expand. One considers regurgitating it before even clearing the plate. The other mashes furiously clearing her throat.

She is the mother and the mother is absolutely furious. She has had such an exceptionally good day. It was hard to get by scot free, yet somehow she has managed and now this stupid fucking obstacle won't bloody fucking move. She is so furious that the chopping and mashing have taken on an increasingly threatening rhythms. It sounds like war.

Everyone at the table has got their heads down and are looking at the plate, except for the boy. He is about to be a victim of The Awakening of the Game. He stares at her from behind his gorgeous clear, sky blue eyes. They are dancing with light and their flickering terrorises her.

It is only because she no longer recognises the light. It makes her feel uncertain and afraid, because the light illuminates her own darkness. She cannot handle the pressure to conform and would rather scream than go any farther. She truly cannot move. They have captured her and if she doesn't manage to escape she shall die. This much is certain. She is not going to die today! It is NOT her time.

It is seven twenty five. The room has become very still and quiet and not even eating is making a sound. Her chair scrapes the tiled floor as she gets up to wash a fork which had fallen on the ground. The grown mans eyes leave his half full plate, he quickly glances up at her and unimpressed, fall once again to their original position.

There is a kind of enforced auto-drive of eye gaze level at the dinner table. This man is well rehearsed in the manners necessary to escape certain war. He does not know it yet, but he need not fear. She carries enough fear for them all. It is burning her stomach, grabbing at her shoulders; tightening them into knots and making her fists curl into such a tight ball that she nearly forgets how to release them. She is not ready to die today.

Slowly she reaches for the tea-towel, making her mind up to take some mustard with her to the cupboard. Every single second away from that table counts. It all matters. She sighs, remembering the days when she was able to spend days just wandering through her house listlessly.

When she was one among so many children that no one noticed or cared when her ribs were sticking out. When she could not speak and gave her food away and there were so many others waiting for her portions that she felt free and happy! Oh, to be back in those days, when she could just let go in entirety. Still though, she never did manage to get the full wrist sized thighs, she just wasn't beautiful enough. She reasoned to herself, sitting back at the table.

"Why don't you eat your vegetables Alex?"

The question stung him hard and deep. The Awakening of the Game, which had started the previous night, was officially under way. It had taken hold and was immersing everyone at that table in its' fully brilliant exuberance.

Of course, we could not mention what was going on, because we were not entirely sure ourselves, but it definitely was happening. We knew that much for certain. We were bathed in the energy of the Awakening of The Game; all of us were, but most especially that poor, unfortunate boy.

He sat with fork and knife in hand. His eyes were hardly blinking at all, he was so very attentive. These eyes were what made him such an easy target to destroy. Their beautiful sparkle was still evident, with a slight blushing around his soft cheeks. Her words settled in him gently and as they did so, his curiosity peaked. He was alert and attentive. What was it that was happening and making this insistent change in him? In his point of view? He did not yet understand and was not fully aware. Yet more was coming which would clarify his position.

"Darling, come on now Alex, eat some more vegetables, or you won't grow up to be a big boy, you want to grow up to be a big boy don't you Alex?"

The grown man had hardly stopped shovelling food into his mouth since his arrival. However, at this point he took a moment to look sternly at the littlest boy. He stared in such a way to terrorise the confused lad, then he said;

"Listen to your mother Alex."

Before returning to the food. His plate was nearly emptied in its entirety, but he had slowed down considerably. That meant that there was at least five minutes of The Awakening left before he drew back his seat and left the circle.

For the circle to be broken something more must

happen, that is the inference. Naturally, no such inference necessitates an actuality.

Unfortunately, the littlest boy was so engaged, that his energy would not allow The Awakening of the Game to cease. So it was, that the enrapture of one led to The Awakening imploding on us all. It was "The Game" that led to so many problems afterwards. It had led to his newly breaking apart and to the confusion of the mother. It resulted in the lack of food later for one and food making a reappearance in the toilet bowl of the other.

It was exactly that that caused so much pain and destruction. It was not limited to that house either. Nearly every single one of us has had the occasion to experience The Awakening of the Game. Yet still, not even one of us has realised that exact moment of its happening. Luckily, I was present at this one and conscious enough, or shocked enough into full consciousness, to notice it.

So there we all were, at one of the most important occasions that can ever happen in a person's life. In the littlest person's life. I don't recall when The Awakening of the exact same Game happened in me, perhaps you do? It is one of those things that's so hard to recall, because it happened at a time before we questioned things in the way you have to, to be fully able to realise what's happening. As children we lack the power to question adults, indeed, we don't know we can for the most part. Childhood is a time before there is a division of self into the you observing and the you who is doing. Do you know what I mean?

Now, I did see a child on the tube the other day who made me question whether my reality is as common as I felt it may be. She made me question everything, because her soul was already fully grown. She wasn't as I was, when I had to learn who I truly was and how it was I really felt. She wasn't questioning herself at all you see. She was so certain, that it was spellbinding.

So my point is that if you are as she is, then this entire story may be without merit. The Awakening of the

Game, only applies to those who are unconscious enough to bear it, for it comes about through individuals hurting themselves. This then creates the space for them to inadvertently hurt others; The Game. If, however, you have seen others like her and been bewitched, then you too may understand and have personal experience of The Awakening of The Game. You might also be a carrier. That is also a possibility.

If you are, then this moment is yours to remember, because these cages are of our own making. We are the cage and the caged and in order to realise enough to be free, we need only see everything. In this moment that I saw, I was struck with such an awful sorrow it blinded me.

I could not stay in that house any longer, because I already understood too much. It burned inside me, this understanding. The actual realisation that we had created our own hurt and through not healing it had perpetuated it in another made me feel vile. It was all I could do not to hurt myself further. I felt it such a crying shame, when we are given such little time, to choose to harm rather than heal. I hurt deeply for my wounds and those I had wounded.

Yet still, it has taken me years to share my story, because in those years I was being judgemental. I was condemning the one who spoke. I didn't want to accept responsibility; I didn't want to have been one of those horrid people who hurt others as I had once been hurt.

Yet it was not her fault, because it was only through her that all of our unspeaking spoke. She was the conduit, carrier of our harm. She was not the one to speak. Rather, we all spoke through her. All of our suppressed pains and hardship. All our hiding and unforgiving and lack of loving and understanding ourselves.

Even as love speaks so too does it lack, where there is no action, inaction creates deterioration, so that everywhere there is self-destruction this lack is present.

Even as The Awakening of the Game is happening, so too is the awareness of what predicates it. So is our awareness happening.

Allowing our awareness to happen, letting it arise, is the most powerful gift we can give ourselves. For in its' arising, we awaken to ourselves and are able to love at deeper and higher and at increasingly better levels. With greater strength, awareness and goodness and with more and more, insight and truth.

We are always growing and we are evergreen. It is the awareness of the Awakenings that are always happening, in us and around us, which shall enable us all to grow beyond ourselves. So that nothing is lost lest we turn away from it, choosing for it not to benefit us.

We are currently seated with the ones who are showing us part of their journey through this realisation. It is such a beautiful feeling, once you come to see this truth. In this way, every single moment of our lives is translated from darkness into light.

Once we are truly able to look at them exactly as they are and for that we need only be seated in the correct position in ourselves. For that we need only continue absolutely undeterred in our journeys into ourselves and our own understandings.

We must allow the luxury of exploring our depths, in order to free ourselves from our own marred perceptions of ourselves and enable the light to arise inside us. Retain, regain, or learn how to experience deep insight and clarity.

If we do not, then the littlest among us shall remain in shadows. These shadows shall become encrusted and they shall refuse to learn the reasoning behind their actions and doings. They shall keep moving without absolute awareness of what it is to love. None are so lost as those who feel that they aren't lost.

Let me tell you something, where there is pain, there is no freedom. I swear to you now that if you are telling yourself that you are free, yet you are in pain, these lies only serve to precipitate more of the same. It is not that freedom exemplifies one from all pain. Not at all. For we are all with our hurts, we are all human and share more than just blood my brothers and sisters.

We are unified in our experiences, in our uniqueness, in our being different, yet same. We are all as one. We are all one. In this sense we must all know of the awakening of the game in one way or another. Whether we are that girl on the tube, looking in on anothers experiences. Or one of those who are seated around that kitchen table. Looking in on our own experience of The Awakening of the Game. We have all been there somehow. Now, let us all return to that table, in order that we may full be with them all and that poor little boy.

The boy has started to quiver now. He does not understand what has changed, but it is most certainly all wrong. He is visibly very upset about this. It has made all the difference to him, that she has stood up and stands smoking, staring out the window. He watches her, as she curls the smoke up, out of her mouth, letting it gently life off her tongue. Then turns, pushing some of what she inhaled earlier, through her nostrils. Her stance is stiff and it is cold in the room. He is trembling. This is coming from the cold, but also from somewhere else.

She is watching him and the other she watches him also. All four eyes and he feels chased. Drool trickles from the sides of his mouth. He stares blindly and cannot understand what is going on. He watches the smoke peter out some distance away from her. What is that look in her eyes? There are no sounds, only feelings and eyes staring. He wipes his mouth.

"Well now Alex, aren't you going to eat your vegetables like a good boy? I've spent all day preparing those for you. Look at what you've eaten! Are you a bold boy Alex? Are you? Eat them will *you*".

He wants to be sick. He feels that he must run

away. This is too much. There is too much which he doesn't understand. He doesn't like it. What does it all mean? How can he help her to feel better? What has he done wrong? He gulps. He knows that there is something which he must do. This has never happened before, but he is sure that he can make it better.

It is exactly this knowledge which makes him sad. He starts to cry a little and slowly rivulets of tears trickle down his soft cheeks. It seems like it is all about him, this fuss. Knowing that makes his chest feel heavy. He wants it to stop but he doesn't know how. He can't move from his seat. What has happened? Why have they suddenly changed towards him? His cheeks burn red. The tears become voluptuous, growing in size, until it feels like he is spilling out of himself. He loses control and sobs.

There is no end to this though and she comes beside him screeching. Her arms are flailing about, but he still cannot understand. All he can do now is to cry. Time passes and eventually he is pulled out of his chair. His bottom is spanked, not too hard, but he is already so highly sensitised to the whole situation that it may as well have been harder.

He is wrestling with his carrier. He too is screeching. It is all so unbelievable. In his bed alone the room is dark, he is filled with despair. His stomach is empty and he is hungry and alone. The Awakening of The Game has taken away his breath and he falls quickly into the deepest darkness. The beginning of many to come.

In the morning he wakes up and has forgotten in part. However, there is a slight feeling of uncertainty. This feeling grows as the time gets closer to seven pm. He does not yet know why, but with each passing hour he is increasingly filled with more and more dread.

When the door opens and his father enters, something seizes him from deep inside. He is gripped. The Game is alive and feasting inside of him. Yet it is only when someone makes a comment in his direction, with similar eyes as last night, that he knows that this is the end.

Even before they are seated, he is trembling. He knows what is coming even before it arrives and this hyper awareness translates into not eating. He is incapable even of lifting the fork. His eyes do not leave where she is sitting and he is wondering when it will all start.

She has taken to looking up a lot, until her voice becomes loud and sharp. His head dips in an effort to hide. The dread of punishment fills his little body, making it weak and limp. Looking up slightly his eyes pleads, but his mouth lets out a gasp. They have gotten up and are waving their arms again!

He cries uncontrollably when they try to put food into his mouth. It makes him feel terrible and he doesn't understand what he has done which caused this. Yet he feels that it must have been awful. The tears come harder and then more raised voices. The darkness is more pronounced that evening and it grows steadily over time the more it is fed. Until, eventually, The Awakening of the Game takes over each resident completely.

All present reside in darkness, unless one day they get to see or face what it is that they have created and put it to sleep. That and only that, shall put an end to it and finally lead to the death of The Awakening of The Game. How about you? Have you happened upon the actual Awakening of The Game? Or are you a carrier, going around terrorising even the most innocent little boys? Perhaps you have even hidden enough to traumatise even their younger sisters?

If you do not manage to bring your darkness to light, then do not feel that your family is safe. For no matter how beautiful your home, or how happy your children, The Awakening of the Game can come. When it does, then this is what keeps on happening in household after household.

So that eventually, there is only that thing which causes it alive and well and the absolute absence of the awareness of how to make it cease. You have been warned. Be honest with yourself, so you do not facilitate The Awakening of The Game.

17 ALL THAT I EVER WANTED TO SAY

The illusion of solidity
Made me bend towards
Where I thought you were

You have eyes like a cat dear heart, did you know that? They have a depth and softness to them, unlike any which I have encountered. It is a very sweet essence which you have too, unless and until you are crossed. At which point, I have seen you stand bolt upright, fierce yet still soft somehow. It is a beautiful sight to see and I was immediately enchanted, but it was earlier than that you actually caught my full attention.

It happened in one instance, when you were playing the boys at pool. You see, I trusted you to win from the start and was quite excited at the prospect, but I didn't really know then what would happen. You just kept on winning; you had had a few drinks, yet were still focused while beating them all one by one. At a certain point of my watching you took your eyes off the table and grabbed my soul with your piercing gaze. Such beauty flowed through that look, I had not imagined it and somehow it caught me off guard.

The very next thing which you did was to eagerly

offer to pay for the next round of drinks, declaring, I don't care! It was a very beautiful flame which you fanned within me and honestly I hardly noticed at the time, but you know how these things are hey, delicately blossoming.

I am very much looking forward to our shoot. I have suddenly realised that every single time you interact with me, you are giving me something and the thing is, that I haven't even asked for it. I have never asked you for one thing, nor have you ever asked me for anything. We are always only sharing and it is all quite beautiful. It is gentle, sweet and innocent and I think that I love you. Not in the same way as the others, in a gentle way, a curious way, in a unique way.

I feel that you are like a breath of fresh air. You are always offering to give me things, in much the same way as you are always offering to give yourself to the world. The thing is that you are quite sick, physically; I can see that and feel it in how fearless you are and also in how true.

I really hope that we get to share with you for so much longer, but I am not sure to be honest. We never really know who is to leave first, or next, or at all really. If we are so lucky, then we may live and get to grow side by side for an infinite number of years. Yet truthfully, the thing is that we are already so blessed just in knowing each other, that I hardly care wish more. Every single day we speak is a gift, that's how it feels, a gift of giving of ourselves and we are always doing just that.

You awaken me to a different part of myself, because I can feel my heart being shaken a little, quite gently and without much effort. I find myself eagerly awaiting our shoot next week. I think that it will be fun and that we will get to play with each other in a very real and gentle way. I have suddenly understood that you are gently shining your torch of awareness and care onto me and I had truly not expected this. It always comes unbidden, real love, to be honest.

However, I am always shocked by it and I am always so surprised by how it hits me and feels totally different each time! I am just wondering if this really is the beginning of love that I am feeling. The thing is that I am not speaking in romantic terms at all, when I say real love, I mean real as in true, which is pure. It is not that such a kind of love cannot ever lead to, or cultivate within its realms romantic love. It is just that romantic love is its lesser counterpart in this instance and also not part of this picture at all.

What has been touched is my soul's heart, if there can be such a thing and by true love, what I am meaning is of the everlasting kind. The sort of love that never really, really has a beginning, but is rather a kind of awakening unto itself, such that one comes to know of its existence in and through, its being. Also, within that space, there is an awareness, that this is in fact, some sort of special awakening.

Which is to say that the kind of love this is, has always been present in ones heart and yet, it takes a special kind of individual to liberate it, so that it can be aware of itself. The truth is that had we never met, I should never have been able to love like this and this is a special and unique kind of love, which I must call true.

You know dear, there are some things which you say which really take me by surprise, because of how gently positive they are. It is like you are always gifting yourself in the most straightforward ways, yet still, always from your heart. It makes me feel blessed to know you at all.

It is something which you have enabled in me, to allow myself to love everyone so well. The ability to be able to just keep on giving myself away all of the time. It is, in truth, the greatest gift which you can ever have, yourself and it is you, who have taught me that in practice.

I don't think a greater gift can ever be given, but then again, I have been proven wrong before and perhaps it is better to accept all gifts as different yet equal. Yet, if we are to think along the lines of the children whom we may or may not birth, I am thinking that there would always be one who is more precious to our hearts. This gift which they bring is one which cannot be torn from its realms of closeness to our inner light. Although, it might perhaps be matched, such as in the case of a pure love with another pure love. I do not know that it can ever be superseded, except perhaps in terms of time.

It is not that we would ever overtly prioritise another, for that would be to cause some form of harm or suffering perhaps, which is not what anyone would intend. Yet the truth is, that as humans, we do have our favourites. I feel very strongly though, that having favourites does cause distress, yet it also causes understanding of our very human condition. These lessons need not be hard, if we are surrounded by love, support and understanding then they are actually easier to accept and learn. They do not then appear as lessons, but rather gifts.

The differences between these must be acknowledged, for usually we are at least aware of the lesson. Contrastingly, the gift is not something which enters the mind, but rather, it graces ones' heart. It may indeed, be years before its' value becomes apparent. This is not something which matters so much, as its acceptance and the way in which it enables you to have the strength to make certain choices and decisions, which otherwise you may not have been aware of.

You know what I think dear? I think that you are like the most open-hearted and positive person I know thus far! It is such an amazing pleasure to be in your presence. I never really understood how much value positivity had in the world, until you came along and showed me. I secretly believed that everyone was over exaggerating how beneficial it is being in the presence of someone like us and I am forever grateful to you for proving me wrong! Haha! There's something I hardly ever say!

As I was growing up, my mind became totally corrupted and polluted by my surroundings. It took such a long time to be able to get rid of it. It is not that I am without my scars, or that I cannot be neurotic and absolutely ridiculously mournful from time to time. Not that, at all, rather, that now I can feel my own value and worth and understand how beneficial light is in people's lives.

The light is something which is so deserving of merit and of such high value, that it ought never have been overlooked or lost. That it was is testament only to how much we as a species have invested in our minds. I am certain that these have become corrupted by all sorts of external influences, which we have internalised.

It feels that for some, there can be no way in which they shall ever manage to "give up the ghost", as they call the phantom forces in our lives to which we cling. I feel sometimes, that we are so enamoured with the fight and desire so greatly to be involved in wrestling with external forces, that we somehow lose ourselves in the pleasurable attainment of the "other", whatever that may mean to you.

You have revealed that when someone comes into your life with an open heart and gives you pure love and positivity, this opens you up to the capacity to do the same. It can also make you aware, as it has with me, of the affect of your love upon others and how beautiful that that love can make them feel. You don't even always have to see each other, yet when you do connect it must be real. It takes some people longer to realise such things, than others.

Time passes so differently for those who spend the majority of their time in their minds, rather than in their hearts. It is not that the time itself is different necessarily, although there is evidence stating that the speed of light has been standardised, which may mean that time does pass differently. Yet, certainly, ones perception of time changes, from that of days passing, to that of feelings, sensations and other sorts of awareness.

Once you reside more fully in the heart, the whole landscape of your life alters, from one of set times, rules and limitations, to one of an ever evolving and opening expanse of new experiences, learning, patterns, understandings, behaviours, environments and their associates. All is new and every single day brings new delights and wonders.

There is something about a prevalence of mind, which brings about another sort of way of being. A wildness that cannot be tamed and a lack of certainty leading to exploration and excitement, are replaced by a kind of belief in future prospects while trying to escape from, nullify or ignore the past as elements that are judged harshly.

I want you to know that your heart is pure gold and your intentions so clean and good, that you never have anything to worry about. I can feel it sometimes in the way you speak, that you are afraid of hurting me and scared of making a mistake which may cause harm and suffering. I cannot imagine that any of your decisions would ever do more than elucidate a response, befitting of the one to whom you are speaking.

What I am trying to say and now am saying, is that you are in no way responsible for others reactions. You but give them the space to explore who they are and mostly, nearly always, insofar as I am aware, their response is because of them and not you, or your actions, or any part of you at all. In fact, I would go as far as to say that beyond not holding any responsibility for their reactions, it is important to pay attention to their responses, because within that they are actually showing you themselves.

The reason for this is that that is something which must be known. We must be aware of who the people around us are, how they are and what it is that they are doing. It is important to be knowledgeable enough to know who we are dealing with, so that we do not lay ourselves open to harm, or misinterpretation.

Although, of course, in every moment we are all changing all the time. This is something which we must also be aware of, that we are not beyond ourselves and that we never truly know anyone, because they cannot be known. All we can do is react to and be in that moment and this is the truth which we can elucidate.

I want you to know that you are beautiful as you are, in your truth and that you are completely perfect. Not that stagnant perfection of which we have been told exists only in order to make us lust after artefacts which are costly. Nor that, which demands of us lifestyles which are not of our own choosing, making us vulnerable and open to exploitation.

I want you to know that no such perfection exists like that which is in your own soul, deeply entrenched in your being. I want you to know, that beyond our physical bodies and our minds which can also be sullied and even our hearts which pain us and can be broken and cause us to feel broken too, I want you to know that your soul as the silent witness to all of these things, is perfect.

It is thus because nothing moves it, it is light, ethereal and good. It shines ever so brightly through your eyes, which I would kiss, were they not eyes. I have always been grateful for cheeks and lips whenever such impulses arose! Ha-ha.

I think that you are my most perfect muse and I cannot tell you how good that feels, as the one inspired by your light. It is the greatest gift that can be given, although it is not so much given as received and it happens spontaneously. It occurs when two forces meet for the first time and become increasingly more and more gladdened in one another's' company. Yet you are no Dorian Gray, the lips of your mouth shall never curl at ageing and you shall but wear each season like a cloak of understanding of another realm.

Throughout your life those who are around you shall rejoice at your being. There shall never be a time when you are not beautiful dear. It is written in your struggle, that you shall always find the light. You are the light and attract the light and these are things to which you shall remain true.

Some things are written in the way in which someone approaches a question, or how they respond. Others are written all over their every action and response. You have no malice in you and I have yet to see you quick to anger in the aggressive sense, having only seen you strong and full of fight. Wherever you go, your spirit shall protect you, which is as old as it is new and great.

I wish you every fortune with an open and loving heart and am certain that these shall all find you happy, well and good. There is nothing at all about who you are, or where you are in your life, which is not blessed. I trust that you shall find lessons within each experience and that even the most challenging days shall bless you with some form of exuberance and light. It is important to me that you think me not assumptive, though I can be, but rather insightful, for I can see inside of your spirit a grace and light more powerful than I have seen elsewhere and I delight in its finding.

We may end up on other sides of the globe, yet there shall never be a place where the inward reflection on your light, won't make me smile and my entire face light up with love. It feels as if you hold yourself from inside and that outward appearances and ways of being hold little worth for you, though you appear to enjoy beauty as most beautiful creatures do!

Well, I am glad, for you shall never be trapped in a materialistic way of life, as your heart shall always be open, loving and caring, even when on a shopping spree! I have every faith in you and your journey and beauty and want nothing more than to make you aware of the power inherent in all the great choices you're making and in all that you are doing.

What I want for you to know, is that the earmark of a great spirit is that it is true to the heartbeat of its soul and you definitely are. The differences between us as people are never as great as the similarities. Yet still, in your open heart and grace, I have found a kind of alternative way of being and responding to the world. I have yet to find this in another and it is such a delight. It is funny how you never truly think that anything is missing from your life until the day when you discover something new and great.

I feel that on this inward journey of the soul, we must resemble in so many ways the ancient discoverers of new worlds, such as Columbus and Ferdinand. It is intriguing that as soon as you meet new people, different aspects of your personality and being are challenged into developing. As if in finding them, they illuminate a part of the light which you also hold, or through touching a space of darkness, you may realise through its existence that it can now become light.

I find it such a beautiful and special feeling, realising that there is lights in parts of our soul which you never even knew existed. I say soul, but you may just say that you become more aware of your *self*. I am not sure which is better, where language is concerned I feel that words may be representative of a broad spectrum and that therefore, it is important not to feel yourself limited by what you may or may not feel the author is trying to say. Rather, what is of greatest importance is how you understand them and what it is these words and sounds mean to you.

There are of course limitations even to this analogy, but only within academia and relative to the sciences and examinations etc. Where I am concerned in writing about you, I hope that you do not find any of what I have to say, in the least bit limiting, as actually, what it is that you have awakened in me, is a deep source of light which is penetrating all that came before. Right now, there is a mini explosion happening inside of me and even the sun is jealous!

I have before looked for meanings behind sensations and realisations and revelations even, yet in truth I cannot find any. All I can say is that it is like the light as it falls on both leaves and branches and all of those many myriad blades of grass. Falling upon them and illuminating each and every particle and adding to their every sense of inclusion in that space, although they are all still separate entities, with completely different realities, of which we know little that is not reduced to language or context.

So then, this is exactly the way in which you appear to me now dear, as a light which somehow causes all of my disparate parts to function as one and be aware of each other and yet still remain independent although all being part of the exact same whole. I feel that this is something which you must also be doing to others, but of course, how you see another person is down to your perception of them and sometimes I feel that perception is all about timing, as in, what are you open to?

Where has the world and its past treatment of you wounded you and left you open to the light and where are you naturally inclined to its entering? These are all elements of what governs what we see, alongside what we need to be exposed to and how open we are and also, often, who I am and who you are, inside.

So that, I must finish this insistence on telling you all that I wanted to say, by saying that all that you ever are, is all that you allow yourself to be and that I trust you shall continue to illuminate many worlds, primary among those all – your own. Beyond that I am very grateful to know you and to love you my beautiful little sister! Life truly has blessed me in allowing you to be a part of my life!

18 ON THE TIPS OF BEING IN LOVE

u touched me in the eye with your finger
hand on lap, and senses open-wide
u gave me your soul in a moment
encapsulating all the beauty inside

The sadness is not grating as it used to, for this time the feeling is more of a swelling outwards from deep within. It is related to her, but it is also not. I do not know why I have this conflict within myself, where it appears to be so apparent that she likes and loves me, but it also doesn't.

Like last night when she asked if Kate Brooks was hot. I don't know if she was asking just to see what I would say, merely for my opinion. It may indeed have been quite a flippant comment, in the middle of her being so busy. However, this is quite doubtful; she's too intelligent for flippancy. I reckon that she weighed up the pro's and con's of what she was doing.

You see, the thing is that it all feels like a courting of sorts. I am not sure why. She says yes and let's do this and that and then away she runs. There could of course be other women, who knows? There could also be other men, I don't want to think about it. I am tired of thinking of it all. My brain is choosing to stop.

I can feel it relinquishing control of that faculty where she is concerned and somehow it is becoming as if the very information she is giving me, is all that exists between us. I do not know that this was her intention. She breaks in wild horses and I must say that I have had the feeling that she was breaking me in from the beginning.

The thing is that you have both to want to dance, to be able to share in it. You must constantly choose to listen to that other person's needs and wants and desires. You must keep choosing not to let the things that lie outside of that dance distract you.

It must be quite solid to be good, yet still flexible enough not to avoid external influences, or ignore them entirely. The thing is though, that at any point either partner can decide to leave the dance, or things can happen to take them out. It is a strange thing.

I can feel the tension behind my forehead. It may be that I have tied my ponytail too tight, but given the feeling in my heart I know that it is not that at all. If she is choosing to break me in, then I am indeed dancing with her. It hurts that she is going to be with this friend of hers from New York. I have seen her image; I know that she's a fighter and that they are tight. What hurts is that. Just that.

I am somewhere in the middle of understanding whether or not she actually likes me. I can feel some sort of understanding coming through. It is simply so hard to gauge, I cannot use my intellect at all. She will not let me! I have tried everything within my power to get her to come and see me, yet she hasn't come.

Last night I met a random director on the underground home. She was so interested in me she was salivating. At one time, indeed two months ago when a similar thing occurred I found it quite titillating.

This time however, it couldn't have been more vulgar. I was surprised at my own repulsion. I do not know where that came from, but I understood immediately that I did not want to be a lesbian who was salivating at another woman's mere presence. But then, these things do not happen with me exactly. I mean I get superbly shy and I often can't maintain eye contact. Yet still I do not salivate, the only thing that makes me salivate at random times, is starvation. When I haven't eaten properly for a while, there come times when I get to salivating. It makes me aware that I ought to be paying closer attention.

I am starting to feel a little better now. The thing is that intellectually I realise that she must like me, right? I mean she has been texting me on and off for two months. It's so strange for me to be overcome with such sadness about not being with someone whom I haven't seen in two and a half years and even then, only briefly. I do remember her looking at me with those gorgeous blue eyes though.

Just now as we are writing this. I remember little else! Which is rather funny given they pulled me in for an on-screen close up and I was in the trailer of the feature film, yet all I can see are her eyes. I wonder if I had been saving that memory up until right now.

So, what is it that I am feeling? Very delicate, exposed and vulnerable, I feel like she already knows me very well and she knows what she wants. I feel like, I am being taught something very powerful by somebody who knows better than I do and that from now on, I will be following her. I feel like, that realisation brings tears to my eyes, because all of this time I have been trying so hard to get her to come closer to me.

It was because I didn't understand the truth of who she is to me. People can be cruel with me when I speak with them of love, so that I have actually stopped. Interesting that that should occur exactly when the one arrives. I told her that I wasn't the one a few weeks ago in a pseudo joke, because I was scared and she must have known too.

I am starting to realise that us, if that can be said, that we exist beyond what we do. I am starting to feel like she is bringing my actual soul to life. All of these feelings, so many, some I remember from before. My heart already knows everything you see, that is the trouble. Beyond heart, my soul recognises her.

Such a strange feeling, to no longer have control over any of what is happening, because you are feeling so much that you cannot. I did not realise before that to fall in love is the greatest gift a soul can get, it is also the ultimate challenge. You cannot but give your all, but share all of your "self", whatever that means even!

We are always changing. I did not see before that it is not so much a choice as a calling. You do not choose love, you work hard and if you're very lucky, she chooses you. You see, I did not realise this before. Now, I can also see that two of my friends are supposed to be together. I saw it in their eyes when they spoke of each other. It simply makes sense.

However, I have written a short story and sent it to her, within which I say that we are actually in love. Then later I go on to say that it is not that we are engaged in a relationship, but rather that we have that capacity. I reckon I ought to edit the story though. I would write instead that we are "on the tips of being in love". Do you like it? I shall change it now that reads quite well. I feel like also naming the book that. Fantastic!

I met an old friend of mine in the kitchen. We had a falling out quite a number of weeks ago and somehow now I have an absolute aversion to talking to her. I don't know if that will ever change. I thought that we would be friends forever, but I realise that she's quite far behind me developmentally and that as I am so vulnerable to external influences I have to be careful who my friends are.

So that in many ways I keep my distance now because of me, rather than her. It is her emotional outbursts which are the problem. I do not care much about them when they occur, but last time when we became closer and closer she grew a heavier and heavier weight on my shoulders.

Our friendship was not a mutual decision, although I am really grateful for it, I am also super aware of that fact. In one sense though I am very grateful for her love and she took such good care of me in so many ways and on so many levels. Yet still, it feels strange having somebody choose you when it is not a natural mutual decision.

Sometimes life if like that and then later you find out why, whatever the reason, I am grateful for her, yet realise we are not of the same clan. I have met others too, but she sticks in my mind because I have tried so hard to make it otherwise. As if making it otherwise would somehow improve it.

Yet, I have now understood and accepted as she must have, that actually as we stand all the beauty is inherent in our difference as people and in the differences between our characters and understandings of life and living. We learn more as ourselves coming from different angles, yet still choosing to be in one another's lives, than we ever could trying to be closer than we are, or more similar.

The actual beauty in our friendship then lies in our difference and in our choosing to hangout every now and again regardless, because in-spite of all that lies between us, our hearts still choose each other.

Life is so much to do with love and so little of love cares about mental discomfort and inconsistencies. Let us be absolutely honestly unruly, unpredictable and different and let us love one another anyway regardless, because to believe we can choose otherwise, is to deny ourselves the infinite pleasure of our own truths. Let us choose only to be ourselves and then deal with whatever that actually means afterwards

19 ON YOUR PLATE

behind my ears, an explosion
and in my mouth,
in either eye-nothing
but blood
your blood
and mine?

"We always had food on the table,.."

I wonder why that was so important to her? Even more important than love. I wonder. I have no idea how her mind was working, but it seems to me retrospectively that it was stuck on repeat. The same phrases mentioned over and over again, perhaps in an attempt to hard-wire our brains? Did she want me to appreciate the hard work she had to do in order to raise us alone, by herself? I'm not sure. I know it was very hard for her.

One of my ex house mates has reappeared in London. I haven't seen her in months, but I can tell that she's broken in the same way somehow. Too much of an idealist perhaps? Or too stuck on words? She could be perfect of course, exactly as she was meant to be, but you see the thing is that she is not happy at all.

Now that is something remarkable. Not to be happy, whilst working, in such good health and with both men and women interested in her. Not that any of that ought to preclude happiness, but I am wondering why so often it is in poverty that one finds happiness? In material poverty there's so often the rejoicing of one's soul in the smallest of things!

I find it myself now. For I have never been so very poor. It is not that I am living in poverty, you understand? I have absolutely everything one could need- including a stable job and the opportunity to work more. I have many pairs of shoes – some of which hurt but are aesthetically pleasing enough to justify themselves. Beautiful and good people are in my life, which is the sweetest grace. So what's missing? What's wrong?

It is not that I am unhappy. I have such happiness in my heart and love in my soul like you wouldn't imagine. Yet the pain persists. I have tried every possible means of getting rid of what it is that is hurting me and have found it absolutely impossible, all that promised itself to be an easy way out just enabled me to feel increasingly more and more bereft. Such fancies serve only to highlight the problem in the end. It is an unfortunate truth that I am in need of people to love me-intimately. I feel struck by this need to share my time and space with girls who love me.

Furthermore, it is the case that my soul is seeking another soul who is special. It may be that I have already found her! Who knows? There are so many women, so many of them, the world is so huge and there are so many chances of either of us escaping the others concern. Therefore, I am not assured, but the moments which we do share are marvellously good!

It is a very gradual process which is nice too, as I just came out of an engagement. I have never before experienced a love of such great intensity. I shall never again, nor would I want to. It was unreal in every respect, like a flame which burns intensely enough to rid itself of fuel, were we.

Apparently we burnt so hot and brightly that it burned some of those nearby. However, it is my contention that those who lasted were meant to last. Those, for whom it was too much, do not know much of either love or romance. They are not real people, not in my world at least.

Things have been happening in really quick succession to illuminate just this fact. In this sense I am much more myself that I have been in maybe twenty years! It is something rather new and different to return to oneself once more. A happening which is at once enchanting and delightful. I feel at peace at last and where I live is fast becoming our home. I am marvellously happy.

Yet still something is deeply wrong. I have yet to put my finger on it and I'll be totally honest. Every single time I get to this stage. Whenever I stop eating as I once did and letting go of life outside for a while, venture inwards, things change. I can already feel how cleansing this whole movement is.

The strangest things start happening when you take your eye off pleasuring yourself. You start to truly see people, even as you start truly seeing yourself. The understanding of yourself and others changes completely as you grow into yourself. It is not the same going inwards as before, when I was angry, afraid and ashamed. It is not even the same pain. Although, yes, both pains were growing pains, of that I am certain.

One is the growing pain of the branch as it stretches itself up and away from the tree at last, in a completely different direction. The second is the movement of the bud into a new flowering at Spring. Where it is poking its head up and out of that same branch, quietly, delicately, with the simplest of pleasures.

I have specifically said however, that there is something deeply wrong. The flowering is not that part, the wrong part happens before the bud splits and begins opening. It is when everything is closed and dark and there's no knowledge as to when things will change.

Yet there's absolute awareness of changes happening and differences coming. There's that apprehension, without suppression of what's to come. There's that acceptance that yes, at last we are ready to go somewhere else. We are ready to start again elsewhere, somewhere else and other but still with the foundations of sameness.

We are always growing and building on whatever came before. When it is thus, what came before changes as we grow? Yet, essentially we appear to be primarily consisting of all of those things which are underneath where we are now. In many senses without the tree, the flower couldn't exist. Yet still the flower is not the tree. Like how children are not their mothers.

Speaking of which I do wonder at times about mine. The thing is that now I am an adult, which means that regardless of what came before, the mire I am in needs attention from me. I am fully responsible for myself and whatever is happening to, with and within me. Which is why I need to find the root cause of my illness. Of that thing that is wrong. I need to learn how to burst out of this bud, before it suffocates me and writing is the best way I know how!

So, here's what it feels like. It feels like I am surrounded by pressure. That somewhere deep inside of me is something dark and heavy. It has been there for such a long time, that I even learnt to perceive the entire world like that. Everything was heavy and dark, even me.

Now, it has been a long time since I saw the world thus, honestly. It has been even longer, far, far longer since it was able to hurt me. Even longer still since its hurting me was created. I do not know it's source, but I can imagine it.

It starts with him. He is taller and older than I and he has some freckles. We are all living in the same compound which has a specific area allocated to children where they get to play. There is also an acre or so of land out back. We are never without supervision, yet we are free to decide which parts of the building we want to be in.

At times, I go to find my mother in the kitchen or sitting room. She is seated there with other women. They are all smoking and chatting. This day their mood is sombre, another jolly, another desperate, sad or longing. I adore these changes in mood. Being superbly sensitive to them enables me to see much more than the other kids. I adore that! It feels to me that I am a member of a secret club or society along with the adults.

Of course, I do not know exactly why they are feeling as they appear to be. That is not my concern at all and I am not at all curious about it either! Things happen everywhere, I am just here to watch and bathe in understanding the exact feeling. I don't care much about their origin. It is too early in my development to do so. I am not yet even aware of him. The one who is taller and older than me. He who has freckles.

I know his name but I daren't state it. Even the thought of saying it gives me a lump in my throat and all forms of expression are stuck there. I could drown in his name it is so filled with so many things. My feelings from those times were so different. He was but a boy to me, I was unaware of myself at all, my primary concern being my mother.

She was the epicentre of my world then. I can't have been more than seven, that much is certain. I am not sure how natural it is to be so attached to your mother, to love her as much and as deeply as I did. There's a chance that it is usual, perhaps I ought not question such things until you have realised fully what I never knew of those ladies. How is it that I am feeling the way that I am feeling?

He must have noticed me first, that much is sure. I was always in my own world and children nearly always happened upon me until that point. Perhaps that was why it happened? So that I might start happening to them too! It may have been to burst my bubble of severe introversion. It may have been many things, but I still can't help wishing that it hadn't happened. Is this why it is that I am feeling this way then?

Yes. Perhaps... at least we are slowly getting somewhere. At least there is some sort of angle at which the bud may break at last. For it must break, I can no longer breathe in here. Staying inside like this is no longer an option, for I am longing to be free. Truly free, without anything holding me back. With nothing at all that is terribly wrong with me. Nothing at all.

So, he was taller and older and he spotted me first, what else? His sister was fourteen or fifteen and their family was so fucked up that she sat curled up on a corner chair of a sofa set, sucking on her thumb. She hardly looked up and she was the palest thing I'd ever seen. Her hair was beautiful though, very long and very dark brown. If she hadn't reminded me of a stray beaten dog, feeding on rubbish strewn by the gutter, if she hadn't have hurt me through emanating pain, I would've spoken with her. As things stood I often stared.

Something would distract me then, perhaps another human, but that image of her curled up, with her knees bent. The way she was sucking without seeing. How fragile and broken she felt to my seeing, yet also how empty of trying.

I didn't understand it, but I really wanted to. I did. I asked my mother and she answered me with a voice full of hurt and pain. She seemed angry. I didn't understand then, but now I can see that she's far too sensitive to other people's pain. She takes it on-board herself. She could also see far more deeply than I.

She could feel and she could see, her mind was also filled with its' ideas. I am certain that she knew too much, but it may actually be also, that she didn't want to know any more. Children can say the deepest and most insightful things without any modulation. It is an incredible gift.

I had a different kind of introduction to his family also though. It came in the form of his little sister. Since those formative years, I have seen too many men using and abusing their women, not to suspect that our friendship was encouraged. I don't however, have any actual evidence and I shall never know for sure. It is quite possible, or it may just be that he saw his sisters friend and decided to capitalise on it. It may not even matter so much now, for the deed is done.

It began in earnest one day at my mother's friend's apartment. I think that this was also in the compound, although I honestly can't be certain. My memory doesn't really retain information like that very well. I suppose it is partly from being so well travelled, also from intense trauma. Whatever, there we were. He was there also, although I do not know why. It didn't seem natural, but it made sense if you get my meaning?

So anyway, we're there, a bunch of kids, maybe four or five. I think four. He whispers to us in the hallway where we had congregated by the bathroom. He whispers in such a way that I do not remember what we were doing before he interrupted us. Only the events that followed.

He had suggested that we play a game of truth and dare. We 'agreed' that the game of dare was actually preferable. So it was that we went into the bathroom one by one. I was the first to go. I was the first because the whole occasion terrified me enough to force myself into it. I decided, that no one should see my fear, so I went firstly. I was afraid that my mother would find out because I knew that she wouldn't like it.

I knew in my heart and gut and mind, that this game we were playing was wrong somehow. That realisation made me afraid, but I wanted to do it. The compulsion to do it grew from an intense curiosity about what could be wrong about it. I was also wondering whether it might be possible that I was wrong.

I could not foresee any eventual outcomes; I did not understand what it was that could be wrong. I was so terribly curious, intensely so and I was feeling that it might be that I would feel terribly having done this awful thing.

I went into the bathroom. I remember the whiteness of it, that feeling of intense anticipation. I remember feeling my heart thumping, pausing, I remember that someone knocked on the door. They asked if I had done it yet, I hadn't. I remember how disappointing that felt to me, to not have done it. For them not to be in as much anticipation as I. For it not to matter as much to them, I flushed red in the cheeks. Nobody could see me, yet I have never been so visible as then. Bearing myself to those kids through that keyhole.

Afterwards, when I came out, I felt so strange. It was hot and sweaty; there was an element of being pushed aside by someone. The excited high was so strange. I suppose that I was slightly euphoric. Who knows? That all changed so quickly afterwards, because as it turned out, you couldn't see anything at all through that keyhole. Nothing at all.

It was the most bizarre disappointment of my life. I felt angered. I had risked so much and all that you could see was darkness? I felt cheated; I asked if that was all they had seen when I was in there. I was disgusted at myself for the pain and discomfort that I had felt. While at the same time, I started to feel relief.

Then something truly intense happened, I panicked. A jolt of pure fear resonated deeply within my gut and I practically jumped out of my skin. Reaching for the not-so-tall boy's shoulder, I said to him sternly, you *must* promise not to tell my mother. Then, in a moment of utter panic, I turned to all of them, all three and repeated with slightly more emphasis now that the beast was loose. We must all promise not to tell anyone. Why? Came the response, I know not where from. I answered, because my mother would kill me. I looked absolutely terror stricken, I am certain of that.

It was a time before she had even started hurting me with her fists, yet still I valued her above all else. Indeed after the time of her fists on me, I valued her less than ever and was totally wild, belonging only to myself.

I remember standing there and feeling so sad, alone, scared and helpless. Somebody who was tall capitalised on that moment of absolute transparency. Only children can get away with that level of openness and honesty, before our minds take over and suppress and coerce us into its submission. There's nothing unnatural about that either, it's all a part of our journey. It's all good! I feel that way.

I feel now, that everything that happened then was just for me to learn. It was just for me to see, that's all. I just had to realise that breaking the idea of who I was, wasn't such a terrible thing. I had to come to terms with the realisation my mother wasn't a goddess. Nobody is. I had to break really, really hard many, many times to come to all of these realisations. It was intense.

It has been a period of great awakenings. I am very grateful for them all. I have lost nothing. Indeed I am just finding out that everything of me, of that beautiful soul whom I was, is still intact. That is a delicious feeling. Returning to myself once more and at last. It is simply divine.

There is nothing wrong with getting lost and being lost. There's only the realisation that we can all find our ways home. That we all can help ourselves and others on that journey by remaining absolutely true to ourselves. This is reality. We have absolute power, but before going into that, let me share with you how dis-empowered I eventually became.

We dissolved, going our separate ways after that evening. It may have been on our way apart from one another that day, or at an altogether other time that it occurred. The taller one turned to me, without hesitation and with a look of absolute certainty and pleasure in his eyes. He turned to me and he said;

"If you do not have sex with me then I will tell your mother everything".

The terror returned again, this time I didn't know what to do.

I just looked at him. He had gripped me. I felt him put his invisible noose around my neck, from whence I would only break free after a lot of time and with exceptionally great effort. Breaking away from these things teaches you so many things. It makes you aware of the power of your thoughts and how they hook you into certain ideas.

It's such a truism that saying 'so you think, you become'. I thought that I was wrong you see! I felt that I ought to be condemned to some awful fate for breaking through that feeling in my gut. I felt that I ought to be punished. That was why when I started to get punished; it really didn't shock me so much. I mean, it wasn't that I wanted to be, not at all. It wasn't that I deserved what happened – in terms of it's being such a difficult experience.

I really don't believe that life is fair, or that everyone always gets what they deserve. I don't think that people get what they want, allow or accept always either. Life is fucked up and we all have our own set of internal rules, that's all.

We all have this feeling that emanates from our gut which drives us in particular directions. We all 'know' when we are going against that feeling, that intuition, but that very knowledge is expressed in each of us uniquely. Even as the feeling is, even as that feeling guides us in particular directions.

Now one rule which I feel is consistent in all of us – just through my own personal experiences, is that of what happens when we keep going against that feeling. Well, you recall the euphoria I had? Does this sound familiar to you at all? I have seen it in the eyes of oh so many people.

They would come and speak with me about their deeds, feeling that they were confessing their evil to me. When in truth, all that they were truly confessing is that they had 'gone against the grain', as we say. They had moved so far beyond where there feeling had guided them that they were feeling pretty gross. For some it manifested in anger, others fear, still others sadness.

I saw it in my drug dealer friend, who confessed that he had let his mother down. The way in which he expressed letting her down was through having broken down the door of a well known DJ. This guy hadn't paid for his cocaine. You don't keep on doing that to your coke dealer and not expect for doors to be broken in to be honest.

It is a drug which is notorious for making its users quite aggressive. But anyway, my point was that he went, he took this guy's decks and his records. This was worth far more than his cocaine debt, then he sold them. When the guy comes crying at my friend's door, he takes the monies owed and tells him to fuck off!

Now this guy is here with me, on my sofa. I have made a point of not taking any of his gear, because too often the girls keep him around just for that. I am more interested in knowing him and his story. I have taken some before, but now is the first time I take some in that night.

For any of you who club and know the rules of partying, this is a fairly decent length of time to wait. Your friend is a coke dealer; you take nothing until you're bonding at six am in your sitting room. He begs you to, because he's feeling like shit making this confession and if you take some of his gear, then he's going to feel more like you're mates. It will make him less paranoid, self conscious and aware of any 'differences'.

You are very happy too, because let's face it, there are plenty of reasons why cocaine is so popular. It feels very good as it burns and travels up your nose. It burns, truly and then there's that bitter and acidic after taste afterwards. Mm mm, it drips down the back of your throat, a welcoming into your flying higher and higher on dopamine levels. The music is flowing, you are flowing and the words are flowing onwards...

So, we are sat there and he has started to cry, because of what his fucking mother would say if she ever found out. Now I am there with him and whilst I totally get what he is saying and why he is feeling like that, it is also such a strange thing. I didn't realise it then, but in actuality he was crying for himself. He was crying because it hurt his soul to be such a dickhead.

Now, it really wasn't his fault, I've fallen into that cocaine web, it was so super intense and so I totally understand him. The thing is though; professionals who know the truth aren't spreading the word properly. People are being prosecuted because of what they are doing as addicts, when everyone knows that addictions change you. People do things because they are addicted to drugs, which they wouldn't ordinarily do-because they are not in their right mind. Simple!

In those moments getting high with him, I thought that I was trying to understand him, but of course I was merely trying to understand myself. I was also aware that he was far far ahead in terms of the addiction process than myself. I wanted to see him, to know where I might be going. I needed more than anything to understand this beast I was wrestling with. It's an interesting thing to suddenly realise what it was that he was actually saying, because now I can apply that knowledge to myself.

I must've been confused, because it seems obvious to me now that that feeling of dread came from my intense awareness of having gone against myself. My progression into that way of behaving was quite extreme. I went all the way into lying to get into drugs and projectile vomiting the very first time it seared my beautiful untouched throat. It was all terribly awful, yet absolutely sublimely wonderful at the same time. I guess I wouldn't really change it, although it did hurt so... it has been hurting so.

Returning to those moments then, for that is exactly where the hurt emanates from. It is therein the truth lies; it is in those moments of truth that I may be released from my imprisonment. Of course, nobody has imprisoned me, but myself. What a deadly state of affairs this is. Yet still, I am here, alive and living and I really want the best kind of life for myself.

So here we go. Farther and farther backwards, deeper and deeper within, just like the house beats I'm listening to as I write. Just like how life gets to feeling as time passes us by. More and more quickly, oh how much more I yearn for, need and am appreciative of my very own space. I have travelled so far to come here and to be with you, deep inside of myself. It is actually the only place where I am truly me.

This morning, I left, I had written up to the start of this paragraph last night, when I became quite tired. I slept, travelling across town for an interview. Then I sorted out the internet agreement for the house. Now I am here, but to get here I had to travel for over an hour. Already today I have travelled for three hours. More is to come though, for I am working in Chelsea which is right across town. I do not care.

Two hours here with you, deep within the safety of myself is worth far more than three hours trying to do that which I have no inclination towards. I have even told my brother that I cannot meet him this evening, when I would usually have done everything to be by his side.

I am changing at such a rapid pace it is inconceivable that I can be anything but myself. I am getting ready to celebrate my life this summer. For the first time since I was a child I shall be truly free and a great part of that journey is here with you. Therefore, let us enter back inside of it all.

He has started with his whisperings, the boy who is both older and taller than I. His insistence growing on each occasion we unfortunately meet. I have been hiding from that playroom, yet he knows to come and find me in this one. I am shrinking. I am shrinking ever more and more tiny. I have shrunk! His power, which was given absolutely without any awareness of its exchange, is growing.

I once ran to find my mother, my pain at his intentions marring my good reasoning. I suddenly became paranoid; I suspected that she no longer loved me. I begin suspecting this all the time now and it has become an integral part of my belief system by the time I reach adulthood. At that time though, I ran to find her in the kitchen, she was seated there with such a faraway look in her eyes. Surrounded by all of those women, as always.

I stood in front of her, taking her hand in mine. She asked me 'what?' both tenderly and dismissively. She was unused to my behaving thus, as I have always been such an independent child. I felt her slightly panicked in her response and also slightly bashful somehow, her whole demeanour then was one of care. I responded to reassure her; grinning with the realisation she still loved me.

She didn't know anything, nothing at all. I made up my mind then to make certain that she never would. Like a soldier going into battle for his country, because he feels so strongly that somebody must defend his family. I prepared myself with these same sort of intentions, I rumbled into my space.

As I ran away from her, I began looking for this boy. I began to seek him that he might set me free. I hadn't spoken to anyone about it, I didn't want to. I hadn't asked anyone's advice, my mind was my own and it was made up. I think that part of my need to refer to others as a teenager is reflected in the way in which I once found myself incapable of doing so.

To be honest, at times this was to my detriment. Not always, but certainly I was on autopilot for such a long time because of the decisions I had made before. It is true also, that I continued making those exact same mistakes.

The reasons are certain, in both my resolve in that instance and my condemnation of myself; I was incapable of speaking outwardly of either. It was shame that burned me. I was a hostage of my own making, my words, thoughts and judgements making it absolutely impossible for me to operate around other people.

Nobody has ever truly understood my soul. No one has been capable of seeing how shy I have been and why. I was dying inside, but because of my exceptional training in how to be. Due to my ability to shadow others and fall in line with their words and ways of being, I remained invisible in my suffering and my pain unapparent.

I wanted it that way, I wanted to hide and now at times, when I am feeling vulnerable and low, it is such a difficult thing because I do not know exactly how to let others see me. I have no idea how to be myself around others when my heart is burning and my mind is in flames and all I really want is to be held closely, to be so much closer than before. It is because I have no idea how to be and what to do that I find myself walking away. It is a silent and solitary march, a swansong, part revival, part escape, part saving grace, but I digress.

The second stage was to happen in our apartment. I decided when and where and who and how. I chose all of those things. I can still remember a door opening somewhere. A giddy kind of trembling at having been caught, but I cannot make out the scene entirely. Was it twice or only once? My brain freezes, it feels heavy. Scenes are flashing. I can only tell you what I know. What I remember. It is this.

I planned it. Like with the initial keyhole incident, building on that premise. I decided to take control. I did not know what it meant exactly to have sex with this boy who was older than I. I had never slept with anyone before, I was too young. I had seen pictures, been told all about it and I also felt that it really wasn't such a big deal.

I understood that if I gave him what he wanted he would leave me alone. That was what he had said and I was so tired of hiding from him. I was also exhausted from checking in my mother's eyes to see if she still loved me. How little I understood of how much longer this same act would be prolonged by what I was about to do.

I did not know then that you are loved regardless of whatever you do. I didn't really know such things. All I felt was fear. Fear and shame, panic and resolve. I was going to do it.

Somehow there were four of us. I think the older taller boy invited the original other two from the keyhole incident. I found it all rather strange that he would want for his sister to be there. Yet as I said, the whole matter was beyond me. I knew nothing at all really. Just please, let this all end soon.

We lay on the ground naked, us girls. The boys lay naked on top of us. He was trying to kiss me and I was squirming underneath him, twisting my head this way and that. Then his sister across the way, close to me, yet still awfully far away. She said, no no kissing and I found my voice.

That same voice which had remained hidden and had disappeared oh so deeply inside of myself. I found it, but it felt so far away from me. It did speak though, it did finally say no! No kissing!

That felt good. Like a relief. Like a release. Like something more might come. It was a flash and lasted just for a moment though. Then there was the feeling of his body on top of me. The weight of him upon my chest. There was breathing and darkness, there was anger and fear and pain and shame.

There was so much need to scream. I couldn't find my voice again. I could hear it though, it was screaming NO NO NO NO NO NO NO NO NO NO NO NO NO NO NO NO NO.

Over and over it kept saying please no more, please stop, please. I have the feeling that I may have pushed him off me and cried afterwards. I have the feeling that those tears finally broke through and started to fall. It hurt so badly inside.

My body was limp, but not bruised, at least I don't remember any bruising. I don't remember any of the physical sensations, except feeling sick. I recall feeling sick and wanting to die from exhaustion and the intensity with which I was feeling.

I remember now that that was the first time I ever wanted to die. I remember now why too, it was all just too much. It was too dark and heavy, it hurt too much. The seal between myself, as a soul and the world, has been broken. There was no barrier any longer, everything seeped in, as everything was seeping out. All broken. All alone. Without myself.

There was a time when I couldn't look into her eyes any more. My mother's eyes, I couldn't look at her. I kept running away, I kept trying not to think about it. I kept trying not to cry, to hold myself together. To breathe, but I remember how deeply it hurt to breathe. I remember tears at night time, how my chest would grip all the rest of me with its sobbing and I would break.

I never stopped breaking after that. There were just no words to hold me together any more. I always had all of these feelings which guided me happily onwards. Now all that I felt was pain. It was horrendous. It was awful. It was hell and I was hells carrier.

Then, the third stage occurred. I call it the third stage, because everything happened to me in increments with specific moments really standing out. This was the third "flashbulb" moment. He has been plaguing me for such a long time now. I don't know what to do about it because wherever I go he finds me. Even if he doesn't, I can't hide, there's nowhere to get lost in this compound any more.

It has become my prison. It has become my hell. Trying to hide, to duck and dive, not to catch any one's eyes. I speak with the adults, who sometimes let me enter into their offices to draw, write and speak with them. I have always been thus accepted into inner circles, yet they also have stuff to do and I realise that I cannot hide forever.

"Psst... where are you Johanna?"

They are waiting at the end of corridors I am walking down beside my mother. My stomach is gripped with anxiety. I am puking without anything happening. Constantly puking. I have never been so sick as I was then. I have never been so sad. I was angry that I couldn't just will them away! Why couldn't he just leave me alone? Why couldn't I just die? Why had this happened? What am I going to do?

I can't tell her! I simply cannot. It's too hard, she won't understand, she's going to hate me, she's going to hate me, she going to hate me. I remember the feeling that everything was collapsing in upon me, nowhere to go – inside or out. I couldn't hide, death wasn't coming and he was everywhere.

I carried him and that awful act which we had done inside of me. It was in my heart, it was in the way my stomach burned. It was in me biting my nails years later, in the delight I took in using that razor to cut him out of me permanently. It was in the pain I felt when I was puking into the toilet bowl. It was in the anger I felt whilst not eating for days and weeks.

It was in the helplessness such behaviours created in me, in the listlessness with which I gave up and in to life. It was in me every time I was so ashamed of myself for falling over. I have only just realised that most people who fall over either laugh, cry in pain, or just get up. It didn't matter to me who saw, where I was, if there was or wasn't any physical pain. None of those things mattered, because it all hurt me furiously. I was always burning. I was always angry. I was always in fear, in shame, in hurt and endlessly escaping from myself and my own self awareness.

I bit my nails because I wanted to forget, to stop thinking. I had seen a classmate doing just that and had tried. My mother barked at me about it, but by then I didn't have a mother, because by then I didn't have a self.

So, this day came when I actually couldn't breathe any more. It was all so heavy. My head was pumping and I could hardly see. The feeling was of his weight on my chest. It was of the world collapsing. It was of my bursting from the inside due to the lack of space. I ran into our apartment, into the toilet and sat on the toilet. It was over.

I couldn't hold it in any longer. The wail that escaped my lips was horrific. It made my mother's voice go so high at the end and she knew so well that she immediately dismissed her friend and rushed to me. She implored her child, a wasted space, a combination of spluttering, wailing and hard heavy, exasperated exaltations. I was breaking down.

I couldn't do anything but keep on breaking down. She was in such shock, the colour had drained from her face and I could feel her trembling with her eyes staring at me. She knelt by me, taking my hands into hers tenderly. She was always gentle then and it was mostly loving touches we shared at that time. She knelt, looking into my eyes and said;

"You know that you can tell me anything, don't you?"

She may have said more, or it may have been a different phrase altogether. That is what I heard, I responded. It was hard, because I was in the middle of condemning myself. I was so angry that I had done this to her! She was hurting now! I had done this, so stupid! So very stupid. How could I be so stupid? Yet, she was there. Engaging deeply with me. So, I breathed and I let it go;

"Rape".

I can tell you now in full honesty that the best thing that came of that word was that the taller and older boy, with his family got removed from the compound. It is highly possible that they remained in another area, I am not sure. I have never seen them since, although when I was fifteen I found a photograph of him which my mother had and I burned it. The fire in my heart was glad as the flames licked at his skin and made it melt. I felt satisfaction in a way that I never had before and it felt so good.

She got somewhat angry with me. It was in a very nervous way though. She was hesitant to be thus. I had become so dark then that I even lied to her about it. She asked if I had seen it and I said no. I didn't care how she felt about my lies.

I was deeply angry that she had kept an image of the boy who had raped me, among ours. I was deeply angered that she had panicked when I told her and taken me to the social worker who I hated. Literally, one of the only people I genuinely could not stand, to speak of what happened. I was deeply angered by the fact that I had said anything and so I had resolved to take it back. I decided to do that insofar as that was possible.

So now you know. Now you know where the anger came from and so do I. We can leave it there. In our understanding and awareness it can be set free. I can also have become freed. That sense of panic can leave me at last and I can feel peace in my heart, perhaps even love and intimacy don't need to flee from where I am. I don't have to either avoid or suffocate loved ones any more, I can be calmer now, I can just be me.

I have found myself in a kind of panic mode with women since my ex and I broke up. She left me like that, exposed to the depths of myself. This is part of the reason that I have returned to writing. The other part is the timely entrance of an old acquaintance, but in a much better and closer form!

To be honest, this new girl is not the only one to have entered since my ex exited. I am very grateful to all of the women who have loved and do continue to love me. It is a remarkable thing when they choose you to love, as you have absolutely no control over them. It is not at all like when I dated men, my sexuality having been a source of even greater shame to me then, given my already being so deeply ashamed at even being alive! I kid you not!

So yes, it is because of this particular one that I have returned to writing and to myself so fully. I need to be able to truly love. I want to be free to share intimacy again. I want to be free of my own sense of worthlessness, shame, fear, loss and anxiety. I want to be free to have as much fun as is humanly possible, whilst also being free to share my skill set to benefit the world of humans as much as possible. I want my freedom, as well as that of as many of the hostages that I can take with me. You may be one.

You may be one who was always told that once there's food on the table, life is complete. Or once you wear your Ralph Lauren polo shirt, your tom ford glasses and don't eat for long enough, then you may be acceptable. Well, there's only one kind of acceptance, that of oneself. Which is why nearly always when one makes a statement akin to the one my mother used to make, we know that there is implicit in that statement, a lack of some kind.

In order to state something like that, one has to have looked for reasons why it was okay to behave, to be, to live as we did. For reasons to be sought, something must have been wrong. I came here with you seeking reasons, reasons why I couldn't sit in my room and read a book alone, without looking for some kind of distraction. Understanding why I sought responses to text messages sent nearly instantaneously.

Absolute acceptance of me, in every single form possible. If you do not accept me, then you must reject me, tell me now please? This is the acceptance that I will not walk away when you are strong enough to be yourself. So you see, I want to be free of all of my own conditions and conditioning. I want to walk freely among people, smiling and having fun! I want to be able to hug and shout, to laugh again – fully and with all of my heart and soul.

I have come here, without fear, without prejudice, without hopes and aspirations. I have come here as naked as the day I was born; furthermore, thus shall I remain from now on! I didn't realise when I received the abysmal grade of 57 in my statistics report that it would lead me here, to the absolute and full realisation of myself! I did not know then that the pain I felt would illuminate the truth, that with my mind I have always been seeking. I didn't realise that I was incapable of looking at the data objectively enough to write myself into a higher second or a first.

Little did I know then that this would illuminate a facet of my mind, that it makes assumptions. That it sought something which did not exist. That it had been left seeking, when it assumed something had been taken from it. Nothing has ever been taken from me though. Yes, I experienced a horrific encounter with that older taller boy. He bullied and raped me; I have felt so much shame in my lifetime you wouldn't believe it. This is not good.

However, an assumption I made, following that encounter was incorrect. It was based on how badly I was feeling. It was that I was a bad person, ugly, worthless, that I had lost my 'self'. I felt that I was no good and powerless and that I ought to be ashamed of myself.

The truth is though, that I made my choices in nearly absolute ignorance. It is not so much the ignorance of youth, as that of simply misunderstanding. I had simplified what was complex. The feelings I had felt were attributed strengths and powers of divination. I felt my way through those and afterwards it was my mind which made me pay dividends.

I do not know that anyone would have done things any differently; I do not know that I could have. Yet, what I do know is that I am not guilty. Neither guilty, nor wrong. I am a good person and I deserve to be well treated, to be loved, to be accepted and respected. I deserve for miracles of love to be made manifest around me. For doors to open into everywhere that I want to go and be. For all of my hard work to pay off.

I deserve to be able to see the truth. For the truth not to hurt me so much that I cannot accept it and for that I need to be healthy. I deserve good health also – not that I do not expect to never get ill, rather, I ought not cause myself any illnesses, such as that of bulimia, or my recent leaning towards anorexia. I deserve to look and feel good, not to suffer for those things. I deserve honesty. I deserve love. I deserve many, many good things and I intend to work really hard to ensure that I get them all.

This journey is far from over and many things can happen. I am grateful for all that has happened, for all of these doors which have opened. I am particularly grateful to everyone for loving me so well. There was a time when I ran and jumped off a bridge in Cork, Ireland to kill myself. Both before and after that fact, so many of you have cared for and loved me.

I cannot help but be eternally grateful to all of you. I also, am here now, doing all that I am able to do because of you and your love. You never gave up on me, even when I was so bitter and twisted. You never let go of my hand. You never let me walk away without knowing that you cared and even if it didn't feel that way, that I belonged.

I have left some of you behind, it's true. I hope that you understand that it is not for want of loving you. Yet somehow, your journeys path has moved away from mine. I cannot force myself to keep on liking you. I shall however, always, always, always love you. Please don't be sad. I was sad too when certain people walked away from me. It is hard. Yes, it is very difficult at times, not to feel abandoned. I know that, yet still that doesn't mean that just because it feels that way, that it is such.

You are never alone, even as I am not ever alone. We are all here on this planet together and if you believe in love at all, you must accept that it is never ending and totally undetermined by proximity. I love you forever and I am eternally grateful. Thank you my friends for loving me. Thanks also to my family. Thanks also to myself. It's been hard, but it's always getting easier somehow. In love, Me.

20 YOUR JOEY

I took what you said for granted,
Looked at what I saw,
Who you were professing to be,
And lightly I gaily,
Danced on its shoulders

I have to be honest with you. It's a little delicate for me at
the moment. I mean, I really, really like you, but we haven't
met yet hey. I mean, what if it's every bit as wonderful as it
feels? There's hesitancy here. You can feel it, but please
don't let that stop you. I'm ready for you, I swear, I'm here
fully cooked and ready. I taste real good too. You can't
imagine how wonderful.

I miss you. I miss you already. You're probably
fast asleep and not even thinking about me at all. Or
maybe you are... I don't know really. It's scary to be with
the idea of you, but not the reality. Not at all. I feel so
good with you. I trust you so much already. It's super
wonderful. I think maybe you understand me far better
than anyone else does.

I'm sorry babe. I let her take over for an hour. It
was really hard... but something in me, allowed her to do

that. I don't regret it. I just wonder what it means. I guess I pulled back? Was it a test? Perhaps.

However, in the end of course I just ended up showing you how much I like you and maybe you also understood something more of my character. She took me over. I let her. I was too weak. Too tired. I haven't been eating, but it's not that. It was her words;

"I'll be gone in a minute."

Why does everyone want to fuck with my peace! Really, subconsciously does everyone want to control me? Was it obvious that that's what happened? Hmm, I wonder. I don't know, but for the first time I've realised that she does. It's because I feel bad about how I and others I've been with have treated her in the past. I've got to stop apologising to her. Got to stop 'feeling bad' for things which I truly haven't done! I've got to realise that we all make our choices.

We all choose to be as we are and do what we want. That these choices, these ways are our true expressions of ourselves. This means that there's no need to apologise, because it is all an extension of who we are. Everything is an expression of our depths.

There was something strange about her today. I could feel her pain. It resonated deeply. I had to wash my hands twice with disinfectant having hi-fived her. The second time I shared the disinfectant with her and when we hi-fived it was cool. They call it clairsentience.

I didn't quite understand what it was that was happening with her. I couldn't actually see the situation. Not unusual perhaps, but the awareness of not quite seeing was. She came in with a cloak of darkness that shall never work again. For I have seen through it. I can now see her pain. The pain of longing and separation and separateness.

I have understood finally in realising that I do not need to be sorry about anything to do with her... that the greatest gift I can give her is through loving. I must be myself and love myself and moreover show her how to love. This is what I have left to give her.

The truth is that we can all give one another that gift, if only we know how. It is not that it is hard to give it, but that it is nearly impossible to realise that this is what we have to give. That is the truth. It has taken me my entire life to realise that I am the most important feature of it, for I only have myself to gift!

Today, for example, riding on the London underground, there was a busker whose eye I caught. Now, before we caught eyes, I was kind of upset that I didn't have any cash to give him. He was playing Lambada so beautifully. He wasn't just going through the motions either... his heart and soul truly was in the music. He was playing beautifully with all of himself. I looked at him though and we maintained eye contact for a while whilst walking.

It truly was beautiful. I felt like a queen! His eyes were dark brown and sparkling, deeply filled with love and joy. I wonder what he saw when he looked at me? I was certainly happy, filled with love and giving him that, but deeper? Who knows.

He's older than I and sometimes there are things which we see with age, which are utterly invisible at that time. Perhaps he saw some of something which I have yet to know and understand. However, we did share that moment. In absolute purity and with such grace it was unreal. My point being that I've finally understood that the most precious gift I have is myself and my love.

I want to tell you something though. It's quite serious, although naturally your love might change it. I don't, however, want for you to enter into this under any false suppositions. The death drive is quite strong in me at the moment. It's taking the form of not eating, I exercise fairly regularly. I'm just a tad worried, as last time I nearly died. I don't want this to affect us, I mean it's not quite bulimia, but it is a reaction to extreme trauma. A delayed reaction? I'm uncertain of that.

It is however, quite strong. I can feel that I may take solace in it, should the occasion truly arise. I don't want for you to take any ownership of this at all though babe. Anyway, I guess I'm telling you because I'm afraid that you might leave me. That I will improve and then you will leave me. Before you came I had given up and now it's hard to go back on that a little. I am not sure why. I think it's like what happened before, only now I'm older. Yes.

I'm debating whether or not to tell you, as you mentioned you were bulimic too and it's better not to antagonise your symptoms. I'm guessing you're asymptomatic now though hey? Oh man. I really like you.

Okay. Here's the deal. I really like you which means I truly have to get better, but I know it's going to happen quite naturally. I don't even have to focus on it. Not at all, it's just going to heal. Yes. I know it will. It will. It will. This time, forever. Even if that's not how long we're staying together. No matter. I have to let it go.

Eventually, all things will end. I can't cling to death and stop living because of that. I have to free my mind of such behaviours. I have to stop engaging in the sicknesses and embrace loving. Truly, one hundred percent, without any reservations whatsoever. I've got to journey there.

Yes and I am happy you're here honey, for however long that is. Yes, I am very, very glad. For you are beautiful and everything I have ever wanted and you are here. What's not to be happy and grateful about and for? I've let go of the fear and embraced love. You know what babe, if you leave tomorrow, you're leaving me grateful still. I've learnt more in these few days with you than in a lifetime it seems!

You must be my soul mate to carry such a powerful message. You must be my one true love to have moved me so closely to being me without trying at all. I wonder if you shall stay and I truly hope so and yet I also know that I mustn't cling to you.

Your journey must be your own and your choices too and I must not in any way cause you harm. I just want to be able to love you and I can do that from near or far, it is just that for me I prefer as close as possible and for as long as possible too.

Yet having said that, it must be that you wish that too, for otherwise I would only be doing you harm. While it is important to me that I am happy, it is equally as important to me that the one whom I get to spend the rest of my life with is as excited and happy at that prospect, as I. I would venture so far as to say that if you do not feel more alive because of my existence and if my part in your life does not really matter, then we are wasting our time.

I do not care about pain any more; I do not fear it, even as I do not fear death. I only ask for your honesty, your truth, for that is all which I can gift you too. If you want me, if your heart says yes and I make your soul happy to be alive and your body less weary and your mind more clear, then I shall certainly be happier with you for always. If your truth is any less than that, than we neither of us deserve to reduce the others chances for finding that in another, nor would I allow for such an instance to occur.

We must both independently decide that we want one another, or remain alone, or with another, for all else leads to apathy and tiredness and bitterness and I would hate for either of us to curdle as the result of each other's light. Long may we remain in season and in taste and full of life and goodness and may we never sour, whether or alone or together. I shall always love you and celebrate you and honour our love and our truth and our understanding. Forever more and I just want to say thank you for you.

You are the brightest and most beautiful light in my life and I adore you, nearly as much as I do myself! Given all I have been through to come to that place of self love and contentment and acceptance, believe me when I say that I never thought I could find somebody like you.

Even when I had I thought maybe I was wrong, yet my heart kept wanting you.

Now that it is clear that you are one of my soul mates, there is no more pressure from within, rather a kind of relief and acceptance and a true and good celebration of life and us. I am honoured by your presence in my life and heart and soul, may you have everything you've ever wanted and may you always be wild and free and very, very happy.

Lots of love and light, your Joey XxX.

21 VULNERABILITY

I want you to scream as I have done
Wrapping your soul's ears for fear
Their inner hollows may burst
with the fluidity of your impulse

It is as if we were never actually there together, you and I. It is as if I had thought that I knew you all along, as if we were bosom buddied, best pals, united together in unity against this world, when all along it was a farce. We were never actually in tandem; we did not really know one another at all, did we?

It was unjust perhaps of me to blame you initially, but you see then, then I couldn't really, quite understand, what it was exactly that I was blaming. How was I to know? How does anyone know such truths, unless through happening upon it, quite by chance? Often it is pain which brings about such discoveries. Sometimes, it is not even pain, it is falling over, it is the very act of losing yourself completely which leads to our breaking apart from ourselves.

I do not know who you are, even now, I am not quite certain of what it is exactly that you have done for me, but I know at least that you exist. That though you may appear as differently to me as say individual people do, at different times and in other places, though you may not present yourself in the same manner, consistently over time, you exist and you are very real.

I may not even ever have had the occasion to know you exactly, for, what you are, I cannot surmise. Indeed, I am not certain that anybody who demands that they and they alone, have within themselves the key, the only true key to that insight into your actual nature, does indeed have this. How are we to know that this is not just a miss-attribution of some "truth", or abstract form of conditioning which they have been fed, before they even realised that they had indeed, eaten.

Not all truths bear fruit, some flow from within an individual and hence bring about substantial changes. Some rise in a person's speech, in the way that they say things, their intonation, the way their bodies move or in the way that they are dressed. But the greatest of all truths, that of whom it is that we are exactly, this is not something which is to be found elsewhere, for it is in everything. The issue with the world today, is not that humans are bad, or not good, it is that most humans are not. What is it that I mean by this exactly? Well then, take ten people whom you know, whom you are quite well acquainted with. Take them and looking into their eyes, ask yourself, do I know you? Is it you who are standing before me?

Or, is it just a reflection of facts which you have been fed, ideals and understandings which you have grown to imagine as yours, but which surely are not, but are both given and shared. Standing there now, in this hypothetical space, you may find a few, whom you know entirely. You may see within many, but the truth is that, many of them, mostly, are not really there at all.

So what am I talking about? I'm speaking about vulnerability. That same self who we are whom is open and honest and caring to the point of no return. Who does not mind the outcome of their care and love, but gives it anyway, with an open heart and the promise of no judgement. Who gives and is forever giving and loving and caring and also, is quite broken.

That self who has been broken down from outside with burning flames, with peoples glances which cut and thwart natural growth and inclination externally. That same self who has been afraid to come out of the shadows and into the light, who has tried its utmost to take form, against all odds and has given up many many times, yet still exists, yet still is real and unopposed and strong and true.

That same self who has at many times been spat on, rejected, cast aside by friends and family alike. The self who has fallen and broken into so many pieces and yet still remains kept.

Vulnerability is love. The love that waits patiently by your side for you to stop drinking or writing or doing whatever it is that you are doing, just so that it can love you again. The love that is quiet when you need it to be, strong when you never expect it, that is angry but never loud.

For it does not need to be, love is always gentle and never suppressed. Sometimes, love is like a carriage that is filled with light, beckoning you inwards so that it can take you on a journey – along the scenic route. At other times, love lets go of your hand and turns off all of the lights, so that it may surround you and cloak you forever. Vulnerability is our love and loving hearts exposed to the world.

We were walking along the beach after a long day at the barracks. It was cool and the air whipped our hair and garments around us. There was a sense of excitement about our group. At the time, I just considered that this was due to the people we had engaged in service. All young crazies, some of whom were able to smoke weed and not get caught out in the mandatory urine sampling. I wondered at how that was possible.

Retrospectively though, I am aware that there's something of brilliance in the very act of getting caged and then released. It has the effect of dropping an ecstasy tablet. All that blood and energy rushing around your mind. How light-headed you become, how you can't stop yourself from smiling.

It is the effect of that something, releasing you from a prison of which you were unaware up until that point, so greatly did it consume you.

The skies here are blue outside my window and there are seagulls flying everywhere. I am smiling. I cannot stop myself from smiling. My baby is on her way.

I was captivated by the waves then. How heavily they crashed, the salt stuck to my lips and I tasted them hungrily. The voices of which I had once been part seemed so far away to me now. It was like a sea parting into two separate lakes. After a while the creatures inside of each forget that others quite like them exist elsewhere, forget even that there used to be more space, so much more. Instead, busying themselves about getting to learn about all that's new here now.

I too forgot that there were creatures like me so close-by. In that moment, I'd even forgotten that I existed. There was just that cold fierce wind, pulling at my hair, like it wanted to drag me in, like I wanted to be dragged in and the taste of salt. That taste of salt, which I bit into, perpetually. One of the voices wakes me up;

"Well? Are you coming then?"

My heart is beating in my chest. My mouth has gone dry and I am happy, truly happy for the first time in ages. I have bought fresh food and ample fresh juices. I know that she likes the real kind of fresh juice, but I do not have a juicer. I am hoping that the cartons shall do, they are not from concentrate after all.

I told them that I would follow them afterwards; I wanted to sit for a while. I wanted to be with the sea. It eased me, held me, made me feel free to whisper to it all of my secrets. I could cry here. I could listen. I could be strong or I could be broken, the sea didn't care.

I sat in the wet muddy sands, it was cold. A plastic bag was between me and this sea which seeped up through the sands and had been there since long before I was. That heartened me, made me feel like I was freed from my own inevitable time keeping. That made me feel like my awareness of time was minute. In turn this freed me from the prisoner's mindset of clock watching. I allowed myself to go into the sea. She allowed herself to take me.

It will not be long now. Oh, I do wonder what she is like. I mean really like. I have known her for such a long time, yet it's been so long since I've seen her. I wonder where she is now. Is she arriving at the door downstairs? Is she nervous too? Has she hesitated for a while in the car?

Perhaps she is even now looking for a parking space. I am so filled with love and gratitude at this happy occasion. I am also aware that the bell will ring at the most appropriate moment possible. All will be ready. She is a magnificent keeper of time and I trust her entirely.

The wetness splashes and spurts upon my face and every time it does I delight! The light is dropping fast and birds come spilling in over the tide. They appear to be dragging her behind them. Calling out to it, dipping and diving, teasing it nearer.

I incline my head to my left, my right hand cupping my face as I sigh. When will I fall in love? How will it be? Who shall it be? My eyes are alight with the promise of such joy. I am not in the habit of finding men to settle down with. I can appreciate their beauty and I do really enjoy their company, but there's something not quite right.

I think that it must be the way that I converse, which is alien to them. I feel that it must be how awkward I am, how little I know about such things! Nearly everyone I know has had at least one boyfriend. I have had a few, momentarily, but it was always only for events. It was always only because I had need of them. After which point I just ignored them, or created some reason to not be together.

I had had some sex, sure, but it was nothing like I had imagined. It was messy, awkward, it hurt at times and I hardly felt anything at all. It was not an exploration for me. It wasn't the fun that I had been told either, if anything it was terrible dull. I knew that it must be because there wasn't much love there, but how to get it exactly? It was a mystery to me.

Nearly every car outside could be hers. I thought I saw her earlier and this is exactly how it was when I was a child. I recall waiting for the girls to come round to visit me, with this same level of excitation. Although, it wasn't for all of them. There were two in particular whom I liked best. I mean, I did like all of them and all for very different reasons. But that feeling, that sense of excitement in your belly, well, that wasn't there for them all.

It is dusk now; you can taste summer in the air at last. Just recently it was snowing and the people of London were complaining that there was hardly any spring. My retort is always respectfully mocking. It is usually along the lines of our ceasing to name the seasons at all. A noble idea, given that people have forgotten that we but named the seasons. They were in existence long before our words and our speaking. Indeed, they may have existed otherwise for millennia, so that to complain, is to proclaim your own ignorance as such.

However, it is not for me to judge that you are ignorant, merely to accept it. For what would I have to gain by judging you at all? I don't think it right or noble for me to judge. However, there's nothing at all wrong in admitting another person's ignorance. That is a mark of observance and true understanding. I am not alone in these realisations; we are all here sharing space. For those of us who may understand, sharing that understanding is integral to our bonding.

They have been gone for hours before she realises how cold her hands are. She looks down and they are red raw and slightly swollen. When she rubs them together there's little reprise. She stands up awkwardly, the marks of time outlined in her form. Who she is and where she's going as unapparent as ever.

Yet still, she is freed a little from having to know. She doesn't have to know anything, because she can feel! She can feel that her ears are icy cold, her cheeks too. She can feel tears pricking behind her eyes, a tear or two has fallen since she first sat down. So, she starts making her way up along the darkened beach, towards where the lights are man-made and her friends are delighting themselves.

I have at last found the music with which to wait. It is *Booka Shade*, an old album full of beautiful beats. Whatever about dancing to electronic music, or tech house beats and being wasted high on drugs, there is dancing to it because of how much you love that music.

There is that. Life's like that too. You can live your life to get things, people, affection, money, peace, love, beauty, experiences or whatever. You can live your life to give. Or you can live your life, because you have been given it to live. That is all.

As I walked up the beach that day I felt more alive than I had since I could remember. Water has a way of doing that to me, of waking me up so that I can recall that I am alive. By the time I reached the group they were wasted. I then remembered that I had lost my cigarettes. I raced away from them; one of the lads came with me.

He didn't want anything 'out there' to hurt me. An amicable gesture, however, I wonder that he didn't suppose himself immune from causing me harm. People never do think that their own attitudes and behaviours could be causing far more pain and suffering than anything external may. Yet then, that is a facet of our mental attitudes and predispositions. The pack mentality, besides,

I truly appreciated his gesture. There is also the harm that does come from 'out there'.

She hasn't come. It's now 11 o'clock at night. Not only has she not come, she wasn't the one to let me know. I had to text her, maybe half an hour ago. I truly couldn't believe it. Not at all. Can you imagine keeping somebody waiting for you for six hours? Not even having the courtesy to let them know that you had made other plans.

I feel so dumb. I really shouldn't have believed all the things she said. It was all absolute nonsense. She was just bored most probably. I've got to be more careful with these people, really. I have to stop keeping my heart so wide open. I think I leave myself open to these kinds of situations, like she shouldn't be able to hurt me so much so quickly. That's absolutely my own fault and now I have to suffer again.

I hate it. I hate this pain. It's awful. I need to make a plan. Plan something which will take my mind off the pain. After this weekend, I'm going to go back to yoga. I've missed it so much. It will help me to remain open and to heal from all of these women with their multitude of empty promises. I need to get myself away from these feelings too. I need to find a way not to hurt so much anymore.

I think that the issue is that other people don't get their hearts involved so quickly. I fall very quickly and very hard. This time was the quickest though. I haven't even seen her in two and half years, what am I doing with myself at all. Ridiculous! I must be living in an entirely different world to most people, really! For her to have sent me such a blasé text message as well! I mean who says yes to visiting someone around half four in the afternoon and then simply doesn't show up. I mean, that's absolute madness. She didn't even think of letting me know!

I wonder why people do such things?

ABOUT THE AUTHOR

Johanna Thea is an Irish Indian mixed heritage, LGBTQ+ actor, model and author currently based in Putney, South West London.

Her background is Indian (Gujurati Jains in Mumbai), Swiss (Bern), English (Pimlico) and Jamaican. She has been modelling professionally since being scouted at 16 in Limerick Ireland.

She has worked with many fantastic directors, including Steven Spielberg as a body double on *Ready Player One* (2018). She has also worked with Patricia O'Hanlon, cast as 'Babs' in *When Possible Take a U-Turn* (2019). She played 'Tanya' in *Red Devil* directed by John Pavlakos (2019) and sociopath 'Jasmine' in horror/dark comedy *Fuck You Immortality* (2019) by Federico Scargiali.

Prior to this she was cast in a cameo role as a 'Junior Doctor' in *Juliet, Naked* (2018) by Jesse Peretz in a scene with Rose Byrne and Ethan Hawke and worked with Jim O'Hanlon & James Hawes when doubling for Sophie Okonedo in *Undercover* BBC UK & US.

She has also worked on numerous commercial and lifestyle campaigns, including RANGE ROVER, BOSE, AMEX, DIAGEO, SMARTMETER, DIVA (magazine cover girl), TESCO, VODAFONE, CAPCO, ASDA and BA as well as modelling with brands such as eco-friendly bark based range designed by José Hendo!

She maintains a plant based diet, due to her love for animals and having graduated with an honours BSc in Psychology, specialising in Neuroscience and Positive Psychology from the University of London, she is driven towards greater awareness of scientific and spiritual methods enabling individual's happiness and freedom. Johanna also works as a transitional life coach with a diverse range of international clients.

ARTICLES BY JOHANNA

April 2019
The Audition Gauntlet
https://www.msmono.com/the-audition-gauntlet/

November 9th 2017
We need to talks about values
https://www.curtaincallonline.com/news/blog/johanna-thea-we-need-to-talk-about-value/311/

August 3rd 2015
An Artist's Address: My Model Mindset
http://www.lampandowl.co.uk/arts/artists-address-model-mind/

July 13th 2015
Digging Deeper
https://womenforone.com/digging-deeper-by-johanna-thea/

July 3rd 2015
An Artist's Address: The Fear
http://www.lampandowl.co.uk/arts/artists-address-fear/

April 24th 2015
An Artist's Address: The L.A. Experience
https://www.lampandowl.co.uk/arts/artists-address-l-experience/

March 4th 2015
An artist's address: let your soul shine
http://www.lampandowl.co.uk/arts/artists-address-let-soul-shine/